# New Zealand

# New Zealand

Photos
Clemens Emmler

Text
Klaus Viedebantt

B BUCHER

# Contents

The southern Alps: a fantastic backdrop for Lake Pukaki.

Auckland's skyline mirrored
in the Pacific Ocean

Impossible to overlook: Maori have left their mark on Lake Taupo.

*Wine and wide vistas characterize the landscape around Martinborough.*

*Otago Peninsula near Dunedin.*

*Deep valleys and snow-covered mountains characterize the wilderness of Fjordland.*

*Round flight in Fjordland with a landing near Sutherland Fall.*

*Auckland overview: on a clear day,
you can see forever ...
The 328-meter (1,076-foot) high
Skytower is impressive enough
when seen from the bottom, but it's
only at the top that the view
from the observation platform
really completes the picture:
50 kilometers (31 miles) of all-
round panorama on a clear day.
Here, the visitor sees why
Auckland is home both to a busy
economic life in the countless
skyscrapers that have shot up like
mushrooms in less than two
decades, and also to a wide range
of leisure activities pursued in the
surroundings.*

The Maori called this bay that flows deep into the Banks Peninsular "Akaroa" – "long harbor."

> ## "The landscape seems virginal, wild and untamed, almost a little willful."

**Actress Cate Blanchett during shooting for the "Lord of the Rings" film trilogy.**

The imperial façade of the **Auckland Museum** lights up one of the volcanic hills on which New Zealand's largest city was built. The ethnographic section of the impressive collection makes it clear that the country is part of Polynesia, whilst the section dealing with "war" shows how closely it remains attached to Europe.

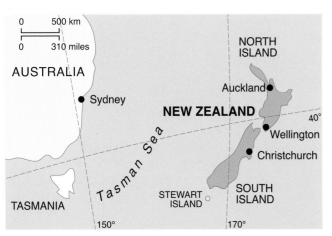

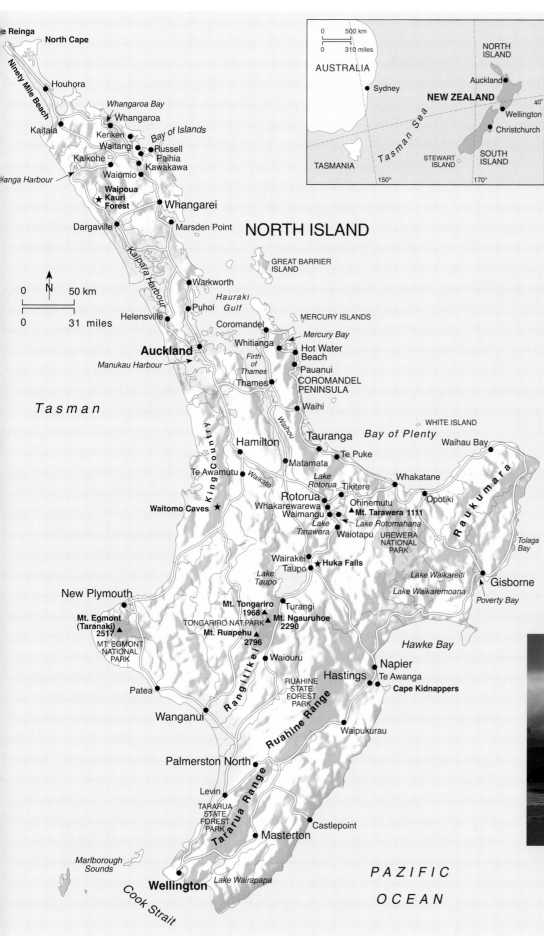

**e Reinga** **North Cape**

Ninety Mile Beach

Houhora

Kaitaia

*Whangaroa Bay*
Whangaroa

Kerikeri
Waitangi
*Bay of Islands*
Russell
Paihia
Kaikohe
Kawakawa
Waiomio
**Waipoua Kauri Forest** ★
*anga Harbour*

Whangarei

Dargaville
Marsden Point

**NORTH ISLAND**

Kaipara Harbour

Warkworth

GREAT BARRIER ISLAND

Puhoi
*Hauraki Gulf*

Helensville

Coromandel
MERCURY ISLANDS

**Auckland**
Whitianga
*Mercury Bay*
Hot Water Beach
*Firth of Thames*
Pauanui
COROMANDEL PENINSULA
*Manukau Harbour*
Thames

Waihi

*T a s m a n*

Waihou
WHITE ISLAND

Hamilton
Tauranga
*Bay of Plenty*
Waihau Bay
Te Puke

Matamata

Te Awamutu
Waikato
*Lake Rotorua*
Tikitere
Whakatane

**Rotorua**
Ohinemutu
Opotiki
**Waitomo Caves** ★
Whakarewarewa
Waimangu
▲ **Mt. Tarawera 1111**
*Lake Rotomahana*
*Lake Tarawera*
Waiotapu
UREWERA NATIONAL PARK
*Tolaga Bay*

Wairakei
*Lake Waikareiti*
Huka Falls ★
Taupo
*Lake Taupo*
*Lake Waikaremoana*
Gisborne
*Poverty Bay*

New Plymouth

**Mt. Tongariro 1968** ▲
Turangi
**Mt. Egmont (Taranaki) 2517** ▲
TONGARIRO NAT.PARK
**Mt. Ngauruhoe 2290** ▲
MT. EGMONT NATIONAL PARK
**Mt. Ruapehu 2796** ▲

Waiouru
*Hawke Bay*

*Rangitikei*
Napier
Hastings
Te Awanga
Patea
RUAHINE STATE FOREST PARK
**Cape Kidnappers**

Wanganui
*Ruahine Range*
Waipukurau

Palmerston North

Levin
TARARUA STATE FOREST PARK
*Tararua Range*
Castlepoint

Masterton

*Marlborough Sounds*

*P A Z I F I C*

**Wellington**
*Lake Wairapapa*

*O C E A N*

Cook Strait

N
0  50 km
0  31 miles

0  500 km
0  310 miles

AUSTRALIA
Sydney
NORTH ISLAND
Auckland
**NEW ZEALAND**
Wellington
Christchurch
40°
*Tasman Sea*
TASMANIA
STEWART ISLAND
SOUTH ISLAND
150°
170°

**North Island**, upwardly mobile: New Zealand's highest Kauri tree in Waipoua Forest measures 51 meters (167 feet). The Maori call it Tane Mahuta, "God of the Forest."

**South Island**, lengthy recumbence: a series of impressive beaches interspersed with fantastic rock formations mark the Pacific coastline.

# Coral Reefs and High Mountains

## New Zealand – "Continent in a Nutshell"

*The sea is always nearby, which is why New Zealanders like to spend time on the beach: taking a walk at sun-down near Rawhiti in the Bay of Islands region (above left) or watching the acrobatic antics of dolphins (below left) – to be seen all along the coast.*
*Right page: the rivers are mostly gentle watercourses such as the Te Paki River that operate on the same basis as the Kiwis: always on the go, but never stressed.*

One day's flight with a jet plane: that's all it takes nowadays to get from Europe to the most beautiful end of the world – the two largest islands in the South Seas (after New Guinea) – also known as Godzone.

Translated from the local slang, this means, roughly speaking: "God's own," or, more precisely, "God's own country." Of course, Australians and Americans both lay claim to this title for their own countries. But New Zealanders just laugh at this. After all, it's the film directors from Hollywood and from the fifth continent next door that are standing in line to shoot their films in New Zealand's own spectacular two-island state.

Where else is there this amount of space without dangerous or poisonous native animals? Didn't James Cook himself declare New Zealand to be his favorite anchoring spot in the Pacific? And isn't New Zealand always amongst the top contenders as the country with the highest quality of life in the respective polls? The locals brook no argument: the creator did his best work here, on their doorstep.

Nowhere else on the planet does a terrain of this size offer comparable diversity: subtropical climate in the north, subartic weather on the archipelagoes in the deep south. Coral reefs and high mountains. Active volcanoes and geysers. Majestic fjords, wide lagoons and roaring mountain rivers. Forests with giant trees, vineyards whose slopes produce vintage wines, and deep green pastures. The gold rush, New Zealand's maritime history, and its role as witness and participant in both European and Pacific tradition and culture. Lively metropolises next to deserted landscapes. Endless opportunities for sporting activities. And all fairly easily accessible thanks to the relatively small distances and an excellent infrastructure. No wonder the "Kiwis" praise their country as "a continent in a nutshell."

Kiwis? One word with three references in New Zealand: the flightless bird chosen as New Zealand's heraldic animal, the little green fruit – stuffed to the brim with vitamins – and every man, woman and child with a New Zealand passport. It is not even slightly disrespectful to refer to a New Zealander as "kiwi." They use the term amongst each other – and are proud to do so.

New Zealand is a relatively young country, geologically speaking. Its oldest rock formations may be around 540 million years old, but most of the country is only between 260–200 million years old and was once part of Gondwana, one of the huge prehistoric continents that began to break up about 160 million years ago. Its separate parts drifted further apart over millions of

14

*The wide sands of Wharariki Beach on the northwest corner of South Island, a fascinating spot of untouched nature near Abel Tasman National Park (left). Things get lively in Tolaga Bay on racing days (below left).*

*Everyone gets together on the beach, which also serves as a racecourse. Betting is the main attraction – and there's no dress code either, although you can sometimes catch a glimpse of Ascot as well (below).*

years and later constituted South America, Africa, India, Antarctica and Australia. New Zealand broke off about 80 million years ago and landed exactly on the spot where the Australian and Pacific plate meet. There is always movement here; movements that continue to form New Zealand right up to the present. The geological form currently taken by the country dates back about one million years – a nanosecond in the history of the world.

Both major islands – the North and the South island – were created around this time as well as Stewart Island off the southernmost tip. A further sixty islands just off the coast complete the picture: they include the Poor Knights Islands and the small group of Hen and Chicken Islands. With its glowing rocks and

temperatures of up to 900 degrees, White Island in the Bay of Plenty is the country's hottest island. The Chatham Islands rear out of the sea around 850 kilometers (530 miles) to the east of Christchurch, a windswept and rain drenched region inhabited by sheep farmers and fishers.

The Kermadec Islands, with a total size of only 34 square kilometers (13 square miles), lie about 1,000 kilometers (620 miles) to the north of North Island and enjoy a slightly warmer climate. However, their situation on a rift in the earth's crust also brings about 100 seismic shocks per month. No wonder that the government installed an earthquake warning system there. New Zealand also administers some of the islands in sub-Antarctic waters, such as the Auckland or the Campbell Islands. All sub-Antarctic

*In 1861, a cry went around the world: "Gold in Otago." And countless fortune-seekers immediately set off for the barren south. Hundreds of riders and walkers commemorate this trek in search of great – and mostly unfilled – alcade" to the former goldmines every March. Visitors to the island have taken to participating in this strenuous journey – especially if they can roll along in a wagon.*

islands under New Zealand's flag also enjoy the special protection afforded by their status as "Natural World Heritage Site."

The range of mountains on South Island, on the other hand, is the result of earth masses that were pushed together at the point where the Australian and Pacific plates met. It was mostly volcanoes that formed North Island, which stretches from north to south over roughly 1,600 kilometers (about 1,000 miles). The total coastline of both islands measures 18,200 kilometers (11,310 miles), and includes seemingly endless beaches and spectacular cliffs. With its roughly 270,000 square kilometers (105,000 square miles), New Zealand is about the size of Colorado and a little larger than the "mother country" of Great Britain. New Zealand has a population of about four million, and 1.4 million of these have settled in the Auckland area. Hardly surprising to find that the rest of the country is very thinly populated.

## Europeans and Maori

Three quarters of all New Zealanders are of European, mainly British and Irish descent, called *pakeha* in the language spoken by the natives, the Maori. The Maori themselves account for approximately 15 percent of the population. More than six percent are immigrants from Asia, whilst the South Sea Islands from Samoa to Niue contribute about seven percent – not including the many illegally resident Polynesians. Auckland has every right to its title of "biggest Polynesian city in the world." The sum total of these numbers is more than 100 percent since many of those asked consider themselves members of more than one ethnic group.

The head of state for all New Zealanders is far away in London: Queen Elizabeth II. But this is largely a ceremonial title that

only really becomes important when the monarch visits her subjects in the Antipodes – on average, once every five years. For the remaining period, the Queen is represented by the General Governor. Although his appointment is conferred by the royal court in London, it is based upon a proposal submitted by New Zealand's government. Real power, however, lies with the parliament and the government in Wellington – the world's southernmost capital.

Another statistic from government records? Here it is: New Zealand must be the only state in the world reigned over by two queens. Despite all their tribal feuding, the Maori also insisted on enthroning their own Queen. Her function is also purely ceremonial. Te Arikunui Te Ata-irangi-kaahu is a charming, well-educated woman who has been awarded not only two honorary doctorates but also the British title of Lady. Her official residence is the Maori National Assembly House Turangawaewae in Ngaruawahia near Hamilton.

English is the official language. Maori enjoys the same nominal status but is not mandatory at school. Nonetheless, many Maori words have made the successful transition into New Zealand English, above all place names, animal and plant names. Further examples are the word *haka* (war dance), *hangi* (cooking in earth ), *koha* (gift), *puku* (fat stomach), *tapu* (taboo), *tiki* (amulet), *wahine* (woman), or the popular *kia ora* (hello, or more accurately, stay healthy).

It no doubt takes a little more practice to pronounce the word Taumatawhakatan-gihangakoauauotamateaturipukakapiki-maungahoronukupokaiwhenuakitanatahu, the longest place name in the world according to the Guinness Book of Records (the old name for Bangkok was even longer); the signpost is

*See page 20*

# Historical Dates

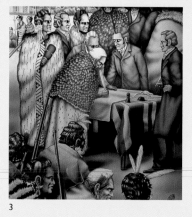

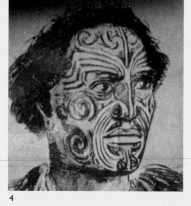

*1 A statue commemorating James Cook, the first European to circumnavigate New Zealand, looks out over Gisborne, the city that first welcomes the rising sun every morning. – 2 It must have looked like this when James Cook (1728–1799) landed on New Zealand during his second South Sea expedition from 1773–1775 and … – 3 … when Maori and representatives of the British Crown signed the Treaty of Waitangi. – 4 The first Europeans to visit the South Seas were fascinated by the Polynesian tradition of tattooing. – 5 The country's oldest stone house: the Stone Store in Kerikeri was built around 1833 as storehouse for the missionaries. 6 Prince William as representative of the British Crown in Wellington. 7 Sir Edmund Hillary. – 8 New Zealand's Head of Government Helen Clark.*

**Around 1200:** The Polynesians first land in New Zealand with their canoes. There were probably various waves of Maori emigration that took place over several centuries. The hunters and gatherers slowly turned into settlers who began organizing themselves more stringently as tribes. Increasingly, battles fought for good land resulted in the building of fortified settlements.

**1642:** Abel Tasman reaches New Zealand on two Dutch ships. During their first encounter with Maori in "Murderers' Bay," (today: Golden Bay) four Europeans are killed. Tasman draws up maps of the west coast of "Staten Land" but does not actually land himself.

**1769:** James Cook and the Frenchman Jean de Surville are the first Europeans to go on land.

**1772:** Second French expedition under Marion du Fresne, who is murdered by Maori.

**1773 and 1777:** Cook returns to New Zealand, becomes the first man to circumnavigate the island group and proves that New Zealand is not the large southern continent it was believed to be.

**1814:** The first mission station is established in the whale-catchers' harbor in the Bay of Islands. Because of the raw-mannered seamen and fortune-hunters who con-gregate there, Kororareka (today: Russell) becomes known as the "Hellhole of the Pacific."

**1840:** The contentious Treaty of Waitangi between Maori and white settlers gives Great Britain sovereignty over New Zealand. The on-going fighting between individual Maori tribes begins to die down.

**1845–1872:** The "Maori Wars" with the Europeans revolve mainly around land right issues.

**1840:** Auckland is named as the

important economic activity to the present day.

**1888:** Katherine Mansfield, New Zealand's most famous author, is born in Christchurch. She dies young in 1923, of tuberculosis.

**1893:** New Zealand is the third country in the world to give women the right to vote.

**1899:** New Zealand sends troops to the Boer War to support the British Army.

**1907:** New Zealand becomes an Independent Dominion of the British Crown.

**1908:** The New Zealander Ernest Rutherford is awarded the Nobel Prize for chemistry. In 1917, he becomes the first man to split the atom.

Britain and the United States of America. The US protects New Zealand from Japanese troops.

**1953:** New Zealander Edmund Hillary and the sherpa Tensing Norgay are the first men to reach the top of Everest.

**1967:** Pubs no longer have to close at 6 p.m.

**1973:** When Great Britain joins the Common Market, New Zealand begins to orient itself towards Asia.

**1984:** New Zealand closes all its ports to nuclear vessels. This measure primarily affects the United States since they are allied with New Zealand and Australia in the Anzus Pact. In 1986, the United States rescinds its military protection of New Zealand.

5

6

7

8

colony's second capital (after Russell).

**1850:** The first six new settlements of the British New Zealand Company are founded, including Auckland, Wellington, Christchurch and Dunedin.

**1860:** Gold is discovered on South Island. The export of sheep's wool also proves profitable.

**1865:** Wellington is declared capital of the colony after South Island threatens to secede unless their interests are treated with more gravity.

**1882:** Deep-frozen lamb's meat and butter are transported to Great Britain for the very first time, giving rise to a new branch of economic production. Agricultural exports remain New Zealand's most

**1914:** New Zealand enters World War I at the side of the "mother country" Great Britain and suffers great losses. New Zealand's soldiers put an end to Germany's colonial empire in the South Seas.

**1931:** New Zealand becomes completely independent but stays in the Commonwealth of Nations. The British monarch remains New Zealand's formal head of state.

**1939:** In World War II, New Zealand fights alongside Great

**1985:** French agents sink the "Rainbow Warrior" in the harbor of Auckland. Greenpeace had intendet to use the ship to protest against nuclear tests in French Polynesia.

**2004/2005:** The Foreshore and Seabed Act provides for Crown ownership of the public foreshore and seabed, although many Maori groups insist that Maori have a rightful claim to title. The controversy is going on.

19

*Tourists will find ample proof of New Zealand's attachment to the past above all in the countryside – whether it's a shop straight from grandma's times (right), an opportunity to invest in nostalgic tableware (large photo), and old farm near Fox Glacier (below right) or a carefully restored old stone house (below).*

10 meters (33 feet) long. Roughly translated the name means: the brow of the hill on which Tamatea, who sailed around the whole country, played the nose flute for his beloved. Nose flutes, through which air is pressed past the reed from the nose as opposed to the mouth, remain popular courting instruments in Polynesia to this day. The brow probably referred to a wooded strip of land on the side of a hill. The most famous Maori word is aotearoa and means "land of the long white cloud." It is said that the famous navigator Kupe was the first to use it – perhaps when he allegedly steered the first canoe with Maori settlers to New Zealand. The name would make sense, as the Polynesians, who are some of the world's greatest seafarers, knew that clouds tend to catch and accumulate over island hills, making it easier for sailors to direct their course landwards. But it could well be that Kupe first reached the west side of the island and saw the peaks of the New Zealand Alps. Since he and his companions would have been wholly unfamiliar with snow, he could well have mistaken the glaciers for clouds.

The New Zealanders have developed some linguistic idiosyncrasies in English as well. The words "bint" for a girl or "popsie" for an unmarried woman are not alternatives given in Webster's Dictionary. Many Australians, however, are familiar with these terms from their own "Strine" (derivative of Australian). Although this is not something that New Zealanders like to hear,

convinced as they are that they speak the purest form of English whilst the Australians are accused of linguistic butchery.

Happily, the Commonwealth's *lingua franca* has survived far more serious attacks on its probity. And the same goes for the relationship between New Zealanders and Australians; official relations between the smaller and larger neighbors also go through highs and lows. Politicians in Wellington for example, do not like to be reminded by the colleagues from Canberra that the Australian constitution envisages the addition of further federal states – a guideline that was adopted about 100 years ago with a view to New Zealand. But in general, cooperation across the Tasman Sea has always been good. New Zealanders, for example, are the only foreigners who can travel to Australia without a visa. The "Closer Economic Relations" established by the two states in 1983 with a view to creating a trans-Tasmanian free trade zone, have also proved successful. Good communal contacts are maintained through the process of town twinning: 27 of these exist

*All colors, all races, all Kiwis: a very young lady indulges in some shopping for bric-a-brac (above), an ageing hippy (1), a beach boy from the Bay of Plenty (2), a Chinese immigrant (3), a crafts-man with his work (4), a young Maori beauty (5) and kids in front of a school wall in Gisborne (6).*

between cities in both countries, matching Wellington with Sydney or Auckland with Brisbane.

Connections to the "mother country" Great Britain are not so close. This process started as early as World War I. In 1915, British commanders led Australian and New Zealand soldiers from the Anzac Corps into a militarily dubious battle near Gallipoli in Turkey. Nearly one third of the troops from New Zealand died and the Australians suffered losses of the same magnitude – leading in both cases to a similar process of disassociation from London. Both countries began to re-orient themselves towards America, especially after Great Britain proved unable to protect them from Japanese aggression during World War II. The United States later distanced itself from New Zealand when the country declared a strict policy against nuclear weapons.

When Great Britain joined the European Community in 1973, New Zealand lost its main export partner for agrarian products and was forced to look around for new markets in Asia. Before this point in time, Asia had largely ignored the "South Sea British." Today, Japan and China follow just behind Australia and the US as New Zealand's most important trading partners. The Asian influence within New Zealand itself is also likely to grow: studies have forecast that the percentage of the population that is of Asian descent is likely to double by the year 2016.

---

### Why not swim instead of taking the ferry?

*The youngest was eleven years old, the oldest 52. The quickest was a woman in 1986 who took five hours and four minutes whereas the first needed eleven hours and 20 minutes in 1963. These are four of the Cook Strait Swim records, one of the most famous challenges for long distance swimmers after the English Channel Swim. The Cook Straits between North and South Island are considered particularly difficult. They are only 23 kilometers (14 miles) wide at their narrowest point but are characterized by strong currents and cold water. Legend has it that Maori were the first to swim the Straits. More than 60 sportsmen and sportswomen in roughly equal numbers have gone the distance since 1962. They have come from seven different nations. Although most of them were New Zealanders, the route appears popular in India as well. Three of their sports men have successfully completed the swim.*

*See page 26*

1

2

3

4

5

6

# Kiwis, Kakapos and Kowhais

## New Zealand's flora and fauna

2

3

4

*New Zealand's natural environment is full of uniquely exotic animals and plants. Here is a small selection: a fern tip, known as fiddlehead (1), a kaka (2), a kiwi (3), a small jungle consisting of ferns (4) and the last surviving relative of the dinosaur, a tuatara (5), a cheeky kea (6), a Hooker's sea lion (7), as well as a Nihau palm (8) and a puhutukawas flower (9).*

"I've never understood exactly why this flightless, nocturnal burrower should have been chosen as New Zealand's national symbol." Thus wrote the English writer J.B. Priestley (1894–1984). But the kiwi has at least one thing going for it: unusually for a bird, it possesses an excellent sense of smell. But this is of little help when it comes to dealing with the enemies imported by the English: foxes, dogs and cats. All three species of kiwi are threatened with extinction and are currently bred on protected islands.

Other bird species that succeeded in surviving for centuries in New Zealand's geographical and uninhabited isolation have since become extinct, such as the moa, a bird that grew to a height of over 3 meters (10 feet). However, these ratites fell victim to hungry

Maori natives rather than other predators. Other songbirds such as the huia can only be found in a museum.

But the remote wilderness in the south of the islands once had an important ornithological surprise up its sleeve: in 1948, scientists found a colony of takahes there – a species of bird that had long been believed extinct. Nowadays, of course, they enjoy particular protection.

Although New Zealand's bird world is very diverse, you won't find any of the colorful parrots there that are so frequently seen in neighboring Australia. The most colorful examples on the Kiwi Islands are the green, flightless kakapos and their green-red parrot colleagues, the keas. These are found predominantly in the Alps and on the west coast of

5

South Island. Delight at seeing these highly gregarious, colorful birds will quickly be tempered by their rowdy habits that include pecking out the rubber around car windows.

The swamp hens, or pukehos, belong to the more decorative representatives of local feathered fowl. Songbirds with special singing skills include the tui or the bellbird.

8

6

7

9

Before the Maori arrived, there were no mammals on New Zealand with the exception of bats. The natives imported the Polynesian rats and dogs that they used for cooking. In addition to their domestic animals, the Europeans also imported deer and Australian possums. Both developed into proverbial plagues. The deer problem has now been solved: they are kept mainly on farms and the venison is exported to destinations as far away as Europe. The possums are still a "pest." Even animal lovers do not protest when poison is used to try and control their numbers.

What the country lacks in mammals, it makes up for in reptiles. The tuataras are medium-sized lizards that have stayed the same since primeval times and are the closest animals to the dinosaur still in existence. Life in their natural habitat is only possible nowadays on protected islands. The museum of Invercargill also has a few specimens.

The 20-meter (65-foot) high fern trees also constitute a biological bridge to the distant past – there are over 80 different kinds of fern in New Zealand. They impart a certain exotic flair to the landscape – as do the cabbage trees that look like palms but do not belong to the palm family. The pohutukawas exert a similar fascination on photographing tourists: they bear red flowers around Christmas and are therefore also called Christmas trees. Rata trees also have red flowers, whereas the kowhais sport garish yellow blooms during the southern spring. Kowhais are the national flower of New Zealand.

Whereas Asia has gained in economic importance, a cultural orientation in this direction is not evident. Instead, New Zealand artists are turning increasingly towards motifs and themes from the indigenous Maori culture. In general, however, art in New Zealand tends to reference European traditions – and especially so when it comes to literature and literary figures such as the unique Katherine Mansfield (1888–1923), whose short stories became world famous. Mansfield, whose work also deals with the time she spent in Germany ("In a German Pension"), wrote mainly in Europe. The books by the crime author Ngaio Marsh (1895–1982) are also popular the world over. Along with Agatha Christie and Dorothy L. Sayers, she completes the "Queens of Crime" triumvirate. For some years now, Janet

*The Coromandel Peninsula (above) is not just a landscape jewel but also a sheep-rearing region. You'll never meet a sheep farmer out and about by himself. There is always at least one dog in attendance (above right). New Zealand wool is tightly packed into sacks and exported to all four corners of the world (center right). It is not the sheep farmers themselves but practiced itinerant workers who will shear a sheep in seconds (below right).*

26

Frame (*1942) has enjoyed a growing reputation outside New Zealand. Maori themes are prevalent above all in the internationally renowned work of authors Kerri Hulme (*1947) and Patricia Grace (*1937).

## Strong Women

Women have traditionally played a more important role in their country's history in New Zealand than elsewhere. It is no coincidence that women here were third in line to be given the right to vote in national elections 1893 – after the women of Pitcairn (1839) and Wyoming (1869). It took a little longer for them to be elected: the law was amended in 1919 and it was only in 1933 that the first woman took her place in the parliament in Wellington. But since then, their presence in politics has been self-evident. Around 2005, the highest offices of state – Governor General and Prime Minister – were in female hands.

Several women from the islands have also achieved fame beyond their national borders: the record-breaking aviator Jean Batten, the suffragette Kate Sheppard or the singer Frances Alda (1879–1952) who was worthily succeeded by operatic diva Kiri te Kanawa. The star singer was born into a Maori family in 1944 in the east coast town of Gisborne.

Since the introduction of the International Date Line, this city is the first to see the light of day every morning. At sunrise on the first morning of the new millennia, Kiri te Kanawa sang on the

*Ideal for nature lovers: the Catlins
in the southeast of South Island are off
the beaten track and therefore offer
deserted beaches, crashing waterfalls,
dunes, forests, and a wide variety
of animal life. Life was not always
easy for the inhabitants of this
remote spot – as witnessed by many
a deserted farmhouse.*

beach of Gisborne – an appearance that was transmitted to over
55 countries on television. But the most famous New Zealander is
without a doubt Sir Edmund Hillary, the first person to successfully climb Everest with the sherpa Tensing Norgay.

In the science world, there are three names that represent
New Zealand: the Nobel Prize Winner Ernest Rutherford (1908,

physics), Maurice Wilkins (1962, medicine) and Alan MacDiarmid (2000, chemistry). All three of them were and are very proud of their native country, even if they spent most of their working lives abroad.

MacDiarmid once recalled a typical characteristic that has made New Zealand so loveable and attractive: the almost unques-tioning hospitality extended towards others: "Although we didn't have a lot to eat, my mother always invited the less fortunate to eat with us. My older brothers and sisters used to remind my lit-tle sister and I not to ask for seconds. They used to say: 'FHB' which meant: 'Family Hold Back,' meaning that family members shouldn't eat so much."

Mount Tongariro and Mount Ruapehu are amongst the world's most active volcanoes.

# Crabs, Whitebait and Pavlova

## New Zealand's cuisine has thrown off the shackles of English traditions

*The New Zealanders say "yummy" when something tastes good – like the donuts in Christchurch (1), the excellent fish and chips in the shop on Oban on Stewart Island (2), takeaways on every street corner (3) or the crab counter in Kaikoura (4). It's worth visiting Fleur's Place near Moeraki – one of the country's best restaurants – for the view: and not just of one's plate (5). Although it's an old adage that what you see is what you get especially when it comes to appreciating food such as pancakes with fruit (8), or battered fish (7). Good food and service with a smile are self-evident, not only in Morell's Café (6) near Waipoua Forest in Northland.*

Part of New Zealand's English heritage lies in the culinary reaction that its name calls forth in gourmets: a shudder of aversion. And up until a few decades ago, this reaction was amply justified. Like the British and Australian cousins, the New Zealanders tended to overcook their fresh vegetables to a pulp and let the best lamb and beef cuts fry themselves dry on the cooker. Thankfully, these nefarious habits are now a thing of the past.

New Zealand's creative cooks treat the excellent fresh ingredients available to them with all the know-how and respect that they deserve. The variety of restaurants listed in the good food guides reflects this development – at least as far as the urban areas are concerned. But the new kitchen chefs also take their country's few culinary traditions into account. This applies above all to products from rivers and seas. Good fish and delicious shellfish have always been on the menu – even in the dark ages of overcooked vegetables. Even today, you can be sure of getting good fish-'n'-chips in areas otherwise untouched by culinary progress. All those regions famous for their local seafood, such as oysters in Bluff or mussels in Havelock, look back on unbroken traditions of excellence. What's new is the tendency for such places to advertise their tradition with festivals – inspired by the Marlborough Food and Wine Festival that attracts thousands of visitors each year.

Before the arrival of the Europeans, the Maori appreciated the wealth of crabs and mussels to be found in local waters. But the stocks that once sufficed to feed families and tribes are now partially over-fished. This applies above all to the New Zealand *toheroa* and *paua* mussels (the latter are popular souvenirs owing to their green-blue mother-of-pearl sheen). These can now only be fished at particular times in certain quotas. There is no shortage of green mussels however, which are reared on special farms.

The Europeans also adopted the Maori dishes of *kumara* and *hangi*. Kumara is a traditionally Polynesian method of preparing sweet potatoes: in New Zealand, they are often served as fries.

5

6

Hangis are earth ovens in which different foods such as vegetables and meat are wrapped in leaves, arranged in layers, and cooked very slowly on hot stones. Since it's quite a job to get this right in one's own garden, hangi food is served mostly in hotels where tourists can also enjoy the bene-

fits of this very special method of preparation.

A favorite delicacy in European-New Zealand cuisine is whitebait, a small fish the size of fingers that is caught in river estuaries in November and December. The fish is coated with batter, either grilled or baked, and eaten whole from top to tail.

New Zealanders would doubtless include their pies on a list of national specialties, even if these originally came from the British "mother country." Pies can be filled with just about everything—from meat, including organ meats, to vegetables and cheese. Pies must be eaten on trust. Some taste delicious whilst others seem little more than a final resting place for various kitchen leftovers.

7

Kiwis do better with sweets: their pavlova is a fantastic repository of calories consisting of meringue, whipped cream, sugar, and kiwis. Nevertheless, the Australians lay claim to having invented pavlova – using strawberries instead of kiwis.

When it comes to the popular

8

Anzac cookies, the neighbors are in full agreement once again: both countries can claim the honor of having come up with the hard biscuits that the women sent their men by way of a sweet greeting from home when they were fighting wars far from the domestic hearth.

# The America's Cup Roused Auckland from its Beauty Sleep

## History and nature up north

"Please secure your tables and return your seats to the upright position. We will shortly be landing in Auckland, New Zealand. Please put your watches back ten years." This was a popular joke two or three decades ago and like all popular jokes, it contained a kernel of truth: visitors arriving here from Western Europe some twenty-five years ago might indeed have been forgiven for believing that they'd traveled back in time to the 1960s.

It must be admitted that Auckland itself, which is by far the country's largest city, was a little more "with it." 1970s rather than 1960s retro might have been a more appropriate way of describing its atmosphere. But even in Auckland, the city streets were deserted after close of business, enlivened only by a brief burst of activity when moviegoers left the cinemas. Beyond the confines of major hotels in the city center, it was rare indeed to find an open restaurant. Public life came to an almost complete standstill on Sundays and even the handful of fish-'n'-chip shops that had taken the trouble to heat up the deep-fat fryers added a Sunday mark-up to the price. As late as 1979, this miserable state of affairs was captured in the headline carried by a New Zealand newspaper: "Terrible tragedy in the South Seas: three million people found alive!"

But this is all a thing of the past now – and not only because New Zealand now has 4.1 million inhabitants. The country has woken up and its three major cities at least – Auckland, Wellington, and Christchurch – have all developed a vibrant life of their

*Definitely a room with a view: looking out over the city from the panorama windows in the Sky Tower, Auckland sparkles as far as the eye can see (above). And on both sides of the sea of light, the ocean stretches away into the distance – the Pacific to the east and the Tasman Sea to the west. It is thanks to this advantageous position that Auckland has the country's biggest harbor and was able to build an impressive ferry building (right). Right page: although the area around the Sky Tower would not win any beauty prizes, there's certainly a lot going on.*

34

own. Auckland started the ball rolling and the event that got the whole process going was the America's Cup – an occasion that resounded through the "City of Sails" like a wake-up call. The most coveted "jug" of the world was wrested from the US skippers for the very first time in 1995 – by a crew from New Zealand. When the time came to defend the title, Auckland found itself in the limelight and polished up its image accordingly.

## Signs of the new times

The most visible sign of these new beginnings is the Sky Tower, opened in March 1997 (six months before scheduled completion). With a height of 328 meters (1,076 feet), it is the tallest building in the southern hemisphere. The tower's panorama platform was constructed complete with glass floors that allow a stupendous view down onto the ground. Visitors can take an outside walk around the antenna. But the biggest attraction of all is a bungee jump down the façade. More important still is the beneficial effect that the striking landmark had on the previously listless inner city area: skyscrapers sprang up around the Tower like mushrooms shooting out of the earth. Many millions of dollars were spent on building new shopping centers, cafés and restaurants, offices and smart apartments. Nowadays, Queen Street is not just the pulsating center of the city during office hours. And guests of the city that make use of the free City Circuit Bus service will find it difficult to understand why natives and visitors alike used to make such a fuss: "nearly as big as Chicago's central cemetery – but twice as dead."

The centerpiece of this rapid development is Viaduct Basin. Specially revamped for the America's Cup teams, it has become a popular meeting point not far from the historic ferry building. Both the ferry building and the decorative old post office have benefited from a facelift and now gleam in renewed glory. The "Crusaders" were given a modern, new terminal and have since contributed considerably to Auckland's lively new atmosphere. In the old days, tourists came to Auckland mostly to use the airport and stayed just long enough for a trip around the harbor before turning their backs on the city and making tracks for New

*The steps made by the sheep on Mount Eden, one of Auckland's dormant volcanoes, are evidence that sheep graze even in the metropolis (above). – Not only does the town nestle between green hills, it is also surrounded by first-class landscapes such as Cape Brett in the Bay of Islands (center) or the palm-lined coast of the Coromandel Peninsula (right).*

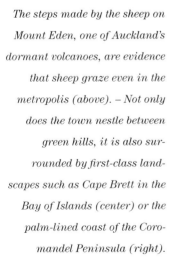

36

Zealand's spectacular natural sights. Today the metropolis has become an attraction in its own right. Its trademark Auckland Bridge was opened in 1959. With a height of 43 meters (141 feet) it offers visitors a further bungee jumping opportunity or the possibility of roped walks across the bridge's arches. Kelly Tarlton provides a very special attraction. The former treasure-diver has set up an underground aquarium in a former floor reservoir through which visitors can stroll down a Plexiglas tunnel, watching the sharks swimming around above them. Next to them, Tarlton's penguins waddle through an icy landscape. It takes three tons of freshly-produced artificial snow to maintain their microclimate from day to day.

The appeal of both the Transport Museum and the National Maritime Museum lies in the way both institutions combine technology and history. Seafaring has always played a special role for the remote island republic, far away and *down under* in the South Seas. The first Polynesians came to Aotearoa on canoes; the first Europeans came on British sailing ships. The first ships with refrigerating capacities signaled the start of New Zealand's success story as an exporter of lamb, butter, and fruit. It was no

*A center of economic activity with holiday flair? It's all possible in Auckland. There is no shortage of beautiful beaches all around the city (center) and the café latte culture is not just at home in the Parnell Quarter (above). – Auckland's predecessor as (temporary) capital is Russell – a little, old town today with an historic church (right).*

coincidence that the National Maritime Museum located on Viaduct Basin became part of the city renewal, contributing to Auckland's new and economically stimulating role as a "cool city."

The Auckland Museum, situated in the extensive grounds of a local park – the Domain – attracts over half a million visitors each year and has also profited from the city's upswing. The massive building was modernized and expanded to the tune of many millions – in line with the requirements stipulated by its status as a listed building. The former War Memorial Museum, famous far beyond national boundaries for its South Seas collection, also benefited from the overhaul and opened a long overdue exhibition on volcanoes. After all, Auckland is the only city in the world with over one million inhabitants situated on an active volcano.

Several volcanic outcrops in the city testify to its geological location. Some of them have been integrated into parks that are

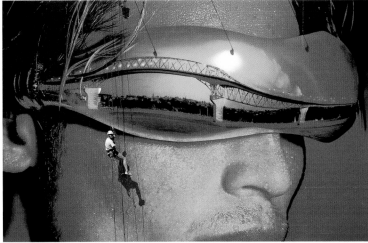

popular as picnic destinations because of the views they command. In addition to the Domain, the most popular are Mount Eden with a height of 196 meters (643 feet) and the somewhat smaller One Tree Hill, whose only tree had to be cut down years ago because of old age. Like most of the almost 50 volcanic outcrops in Auckland, both of these hills were once extended by the Maori into fortified settlements, or so-called *pas*.

The volcanoes are "dormant" and have been for several thousand years. However, scientists have calculated that about 5 percent of Auckland's volcanoes could become active again within the next 50 years – a terrible prospect for the densely populated city. The oldest fire mountains developed around 140,000 years ago, the youngest volcano is only about 600 years old: the island of Rangitoto in the Hauraki Gulf.

This youngest of the more than 30 islands in the Hauraki Gulf is a popular destination for day-trippers. This also applies to the second biggest island in the archipelago after Great Barrier –

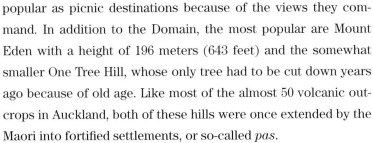

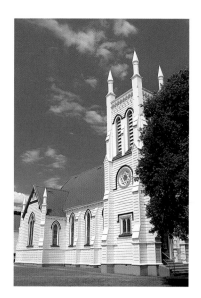

Waiheke Island, which can be reached by a roughly 30-minute ferry-trip from Auckland city and is becoming increasingly popular as a lifestyle colony. The Maori were the first to discover the advantages of island life – although they remained more concerned with military considerations than comfort. Just as the easily fortifiable volcanic outcrops in the city provided strategic vantage points, so too did the islands. The same applied to the 2-kilometer (1.2-mile) wide strip of land between the Tasman Sea and the Pacific on which Auckland is situated. The European settlers also appreciated this position: as early as 1840, they relocated their capital from Russell to the more accessible Auckland. That this function was transferred to Wellington twenty-five years later in 1865 must be put down to this city's proximity to South Island, on which there were rumblings about the foundation of an independent state. Ever since that time, Aucklanders have complained with some justification that they are ruled by bureaucrats some 700 miles away – despite the fact that their city is the country's real metropolis.

## Majestic tree giants

Naturally, this applies to an even greater degree to the northern part of the country – somewhat unimaginatively called Northland. It's about 400 kilometers (250 miles) from Auckland to Cape Reinga situated at the tip of the long, narrow stretch of country – more than six hours drive according to the website of the AA automobile club.

Clearly, one should set aside more than just a day for a trip through Northland – not least because this peninsula, with its bays, beaches, and forests, has some really spectacular sights in store for the visitor. As the birthplace of "white" New Zealand, it also has a very special historical relevance that manifests itself right up to the present day. Not that the white settlers left a purely positive legacy: the few remaining tree trunks in the formerly majestic Kauri Forests testify to the European greed for the wood provided by these trees, which are some of the tallest in the world. For the seafarers, wood from Kauris was almost as valuable as gold: ideal for

masts and perfect for constructing ships, building houses – and for export purposes. So it did not take long for the trees to come down – as the Kauri Museum in Matakohe makes clear. The record is held to this day by one particularly fine specimen, felled in 1850 with a girth of 23.43 meters (76.87 feet). Thankfully, the "God of the Forest" survived this phase: Tane Mahuta near Waipoua is nearly 52 meters (171 feet) high and about 1,200 years old. His successor is already staking his claim in Whangarei with a girth of 20 meters (66 feet). But Tane Mahuta could get even bigger: Kauris live and continue to grow for 2,000 years.

When so many Kauri trees had been cut down that they could no longer be relied upon as a viable export commodity, some resourceful settlers discovered that that the gum or resin from Kauri trees could be used for the production of lacquer. The forests were scoured for hardened lumps of this gum and trees were tapped for a fresh supply. The highly profitable business only came to an end when industrial production of cheaper synthetic chemicals got underway.

*See page 46*

The Bay of Islands has over 150 islands and many more bays.

# Always Close to the Wind

## Sailing: New Zealand's national pastime

1

2

*Whether it's on a racing yacht in Auckland (1 and 2), a children's mini-boat outside Wellington (4), a catamaran on Lake Wanaka (5) or with friends in the Bay of Islands (3): where water and wind come together, so do the Kiwis and their sailing boats. Frequent companions: dolphins such as those in the Bay of Islands (6).*

3

4

"I am sailing": nobody intones Rod Stewart's hit with more fervor than New Zealanders and there are always some of them around to receive a medal at major sailing events. On one occasion, after sportsmen from down under had crossed the line ahead of all the others once again, a disgruntled rival was overheard complaining that: "Maybe Kiwis can't fly, but they're dammed good sailors."

A look at the trophy collections in the clubhouses from Auckland to Invercargill is proof enough of this proficiency: the most prestigious sailing event, the America's Cup, has been won twice by a team from New Zealand. First prize in the toughest race, the Whitbread Race (Volvo Ocean Race) around the

44

5

6

world, has been awarded three times to New Zealand's colors. And the ten medals that have been won at summer games – plus over sixty world records – add up to make sailing the most successful Olympic discipline in the island state

The international triumphs celebrated by this modestly populated country would be unthinkable if sailing were an elitist sport and not a national pastime. It is often said that there are more sailing boats per capita here than anywhere else in the world. Although this is difficult to prove, anybody looking out over Auckland – the "City of Sails" – and its two marine bays on any given weekend blessed with good weather will feel inclined to endorse the probability of this world record. Mind you, the inhabitants of Wellington are just as inclined to assert that they have even more boats than the Aucklanders ...

Where does this national passion for canvas and wind come from? Harold Bennett of the Royal New Zealand Yacht Squadron believes that its origins are manifold: "Dedication from childhood onwards, constant and intense competition in native waters, an extremely competent maritime industry that actively supports sailors – these factors all play a role. But a lot also has to do simply with geography. As an island state, New Zealand has deep-seated maritime traditions." Bennett points out that both the Maori and the European settlers only reached their destinations after lengthy journeys across the seas: "A long period of dependency on the ocean for any kind of trade and for all forms of communication forced New Zealanders to build reliable, seaworthy ships and acquire immediate knowledge of seafaring and shipping." New Zealand's shipbuilders are just as much in demand worldwide as the country's sailors are proficient at amassing the great regatta prizes. The best example is Russell Coutts. The Olympic Sailing

Champion won the "auld mug" three times in a row. The first two times, he sailed under New Zealand's flag. On the third occasion, he entered the race for Switzerland – and has since been regarded as a traitor by the Kiwis. In the meantime, New Zealand has set up a support program for talented young sailors: there are over 100 sailing clubs in the country and anyone who shows promise is invited to take part in special training courses. Help also comes from the so-called P class – a local invention. The small dinghies are notably difficult to sail but for many young Kiwis they are simply a logical intermediate step between tricycle and boat. And because the P class boat really presents a challenge to teenagers at the helm, they find themselves well prepared when they do advance to keel boats.

Several reforestation and horticultural breeding programs are currently being operated in Northland. The young Kauris do well in the subtropical climate, especially since the trees grow quickly during the first years of their lives – despite their extreme longevity. Kauri wood is rare and therefore expensive. Nowadays, it is only used for the production of furniture and souvenirs. Occasionally, Maori use the bigger trunks to build so-called one-tree canoes, using a technique inherited from their ancestors.

In former times, the beaches on Northland were used as points of departure for the export of tree trunks. Today, they are used exclusively for leisure activities – with one exception: the famous 90-Mile-Beach on the west coast has such a firm, sandy underground that it can be used during low tide as an alternative to the only road going in a northerly direction. Tourists are especially keen to roll along the sandy thoroughfare in their buses – and they don't mind if the going gets a little rougher than usual: in point of fact, this strip of sand is only 64 and not 90 miles long. Measuring the distance in kilometers – a total of 103 – makes the surfer's favorite stretch of sand sound a little more impressive.

Those that extol Cape Reinga is the northernmost point of New Zealand's mainland are also guilty of misrepresentation: Surville Cliffs are situated about 5 kilometers (3 miles) away and are actually further north, geographically speaking. But Cape Reinga has more to offer. Not only is it easily accessibly by road, it is also more photogenic – thanks to a lighthouse that is visible from a distance of 50 kilometers (30 miles). And last, but definitely not least, it is also home to an ancient, gnarled Pohutuka tree with an estimated age of 800 years that is of great spiritual significance for the Maori. They believe that this is where the souls of the dead leave dry land, drift over the sea to the Three Kings Islands where they look back one last time onto New Zealand before they finally descend into the depths of the ocean on their way to Hawaiki, the spiritual hereafter.

## Retracing history's footprints on the beach

On the way back south, it's a good idea to stop for a swim on the beaches of Doubtless Bay. And no visitor should pass up the opportunity to call in on the Bay of Islands, whose 140 islets more than justify its name. This sunken river system is impressive not only by virtue of its natural beauty. Many of the bay's notable sights must be put down to history. This is where Samuel Marsden founded four mission stations from the year 1814. After 1820, Kororareka (today's Russell) was also the site of a less salubrious settlement inhabited by society's less desirable elements: sailors who had deserted, freed prisoners from Australia, uncouth whale catchers, distillers of whisky, and Maori "ship-girls" – all of whom made sure that the place more than lived up to its nickname as "Hellhole of the Pacific."

The 1840 Treaty of Waitangi promised change. Most of the important Maori chiefs came to the house of one James Busby, the official representative of the British Crown (known as the British Resident), to sign a document that transferred all sovereign rights over New Zealand to Great Britain. It is doubtful that they were all fully aware of what they were signing and Maori activists continue to question the Treaty's validity up to the present day. "Treaty House" with its beautiful terrace view over the Bay, has been preserved and turned into a museum. For a few months of that same year, Kororareka – renamed Russell in an effort to shake off its bad reputation – acted as the country's capital.

Four years later, the treaty's first signatory, Chief Hone Heke, instigated a rebellion against the British that centered above all on land rights. This was the starting shot for the Maori wars, which quickly spread to other parts of the country and lasted until 1870. Heke's rebellion ended with a British victory although his troops had burned down Russell just twelve months earlier. Christ Church, the oldest church in the country, still bears the scars of the fierce fighting.

What a contrast: today, the Bay of Islands is a particularly peaceful corner of New Zealand. Conflict is restricted to tourists squabbling over the best restaurant seating during the main Christmas season in Paihia. Several boat trips through the attractive area start here from the pier. The boats are often accompanied by dolphins – and sometimes the odd whale or shark puts in a distant appearance. Most of the Bay of Islands is a protected maritime park. The tours generally go no further than Cape Brett at the Bay's exit, where the easternmost tip of land is embellished by a little rocky island with a big hole through which the boats pass before turning back towards the harbor. The "Hole-in-the-

*Left page: It is not just the beautiful coastline that attracts visitors to Matauri Bay. Divers also love the bay in which the "Rainbow Warrior" was sunk. Horse or seahorse? Riders on the Northland beaches sometimes seem confused (left).*

*In the colony's early days, the small town of Russell – known for its ruffians, whores, and escaped prisoners – was also known as the "Hellhole of the Pacific" (center). It's worth driving northwards to Cape Reinga – and not only for the trip over 90-Mile-Beach on which even camper vans are permitted.*

47

*Which camper van tourist would want to pass up the Northland region (right) with natural scenery such as the deep Bay of Hokianga Harbour (large photo) or the short Te-Paki River (below)?*

Rock" is also part of the popular "Cream Trip" – a boat tour that functions as a postal service for some of the islands' inhabitants or those living on particularly remote parts of the bay coastline. The tour got its name from the milk chums that the captain used to pick up from the remote farms whilst he was delivering the mail. Today, the transport of tourists is the main line of business – including afternoon tea – a cream tea, of course.

Tea was probably not the beverage of choice during New Zealand's first gold rush, which broke out in the mid-19th century on the Coromandel Peninsula. It was a short-lived affair and the peninsula to the east of Auckland – and with it, the Hauraki Gulf – soon sank back into its customary calm.

During the off-season at least, the area remains quiet, despite the region's proximity to the economic metropolis Auckland.

When the nation goes on vacation, then life starts pulsating in the normally reclusive seaside resorts such as Pauanui, Tairua, or Whangamata. In addition, more and more Aucklanders are discovering the charms of the peninsula – originally named after a ship – and are building themselves vacation homes on the coastal segments above the beach.

There is no reason to anticipate a pervasive urban sprawl, however, since large sections of the coast are rocky, beaten by waves, and barely accessible. The mountainous interior lacks infrastructure and appears as wild and lonely as it ever was. Only the lack of tall Kauri trees in the woods serves to remind posterity that people passed through here at all: wood pillagers did just as thorough a job here in the early 19th century as their fellow marauders in Northland.

Today, it is above all artists and artisans who live on Coromandel: potters, weavers, painters, and others who enjoy welcoming visitors into their studios. Some jewelry designers have specialized in working with local semi-precious stones – of which Coromandel has a great variety on offer. Agate and crystal quartz were once mined here on the peninsula.

The colorful stones are also a product of the local geological heritage – the volcanoes that formed the headland. There is plenty more evidence that the earth still sizzles here on Hot Water Beach and Mercury Bay where warm water constantly bubbles up through the sand. When the tide goes out, visitors dig themselves a hole in which they can relax in their own private bath. There's no better or more appropriate preparation for a visit in the hot heart of New Zealand: Rotorua.

Pristine Beauty – Cape Maria van Diemen and Cape Reinga.

# All in Black

## Why it's "all black" for (nearly) all the sports

*1 For daredevils: bungee jumping off the Kawaru Bridge near Queenstown. – 2 The New Zealand rugby team, the "All Blacks" (in black!), present their traditional* haka *(Maori dance). Tonga's national team (in red) returns the salute. – 3 Fly fishing on Lake Taupo. – 4 "Sky diving" on the west coast. – 5 Whitewater rafting near Queenstown. 6 Long-distance cycle path on the west coast. – 7 Take a canoe out on the Green Lake near Rotorua. 8 Practice makes perfect – never truer than when it comes to New Zealand's national sport cricket.*

The so-called "All Blacks," New Zealand's rugby team, enjoy an almost cult status in their country. Perhaps this is why their black jerseys, decorated with a silver fern leaf, have become the fashion icon for nearly all New Zealand's national sports teams.

Regardless of discipline, the Kiwi sportspeople prefer black. It seems as though this tradition might actually be founded on an error. When a Kiwi team visiting Great Britain in 1905 proved itself victorious time and time again, an English newspaper is reputed to have expressed the nation's concern at its serial defeat by describing how the local team had only ever seen "all backs" of their faster opponents. Later, a printing error turned this in "all blacks." But this version of the phrase's etymology is contentious: the website of the Rugby www.rugby-museum.co.nz deals extensively with this issue.

6

7

8

5

Whatever the case, rugby is clearly New Zealand's most popular sport, more popular even than cricket and sailing. All other kinds of competition trail far behind this triumvirate – including soccer, which tends to be the number one sport in most countries with a British background.

The soccer players have come to terms with their subsidiary role and have volunteered to take a back seat – even going so far as to call themselves the "All Whites." But soccer remains the sport with the most active players – probably because many girls enjoy running after the ball more than getting dirty in the often rough and ready scramble of rugby. Women's rugby, represented by the ladies Black Ferns team, is not particularly popular.

When the rugby heroes take a break during the summer, cricket takes on the role of most popular sport. Internationally, however, the gentlemen in their "whites" are less successful than the rugby stars: it was only in 1956 that they won their first international game.

New Zealand's ladies are very successful when it comes to netball – and this is also the most popular women's sport, and the second-most popular sport amongst girls (after swimming). Men tend to enjoy golf – a sport that is not considered elitist in New Zealand. And it doesn't cost much to get out and swing that golf club: green fees in some clubs are under 10 dollars. Of the 400 or so golf courses in New Zealand, the nearest is never further than 45 minutes drive away. Seen in terms of a per capita distribution, that's a world record. All the more astonishing that the Kiwis have never produced a world star in this game.

Whilst orienteering tends to be something of a specialist sport in other countries, there is no shortage of sports enthusiasts in New Zealand who enjoy going out into the wilds and practicing their running and orientation skills. Internationally, the Kiwi orienteering enthusiasts prefer the contests with their Australian neighbors, the "Bushrangers." The Kiwi team calls itself "Pinestars" – an innocuous name. New Zealand's badminton players were slightly more audacious. They wanted to name their national team "Black Cocks" – all puns fully intended. Although the name was never officially sanctioned and remains contentious, it quickly established itself as the unofficial designation – a condom manufacturer has already suggested a sponsoring contract.

# Where the Earth Moves

## The fascinating world of geysers and volcanoes on North Island

Whoosh! The column of water shoots 17 meters (56 feet) out of the earth's interior with a small explosion. Not bad today but still, nowhere close to the record. On good days, Lady Knox manages a height of about 20 meters (around 65 feet). But the lady needs some help from a bar of soap – it loosens the surface tension on the water and turns the hot water holes in and around Rotorua into genuine geysers. The ritual has the huge advantage of re-occurring punctually every day around 10.15 a.m. especially for the tourists who have gathered for the spectacle.

Visitors from all around the world can now appreciate this attraction – thanks to the fact that New Zealand once used the area as an "open prison" for petty criminals and the young men who decided to wash their trousers in the water hole and discovered that soap triggers geysers. This was not enough to attract visitors since the water hole was far too large. So the prison guard had the bright idea of ordering the prisoners to make the hole smaller by filling it up with large stones – and the hot fountain was born. Lord Ranfurly, the Governor of the colony of New Zealand, visited the jail in 1903 – a suitable occasion to name the geyser after his daughter, Constance Knox.

Today, the lady helps keep the cash flow spouting in Waiotapu ("Holy Water"), a government-owned nature reserve not far from the capital city of the active volcano region in the center of North Island. With its craters, its pools of blubbering mud, and its red-rimmed "champagne pool," Waiotapu is the most colorful of Rotorua's thermal areas. The most active is Tikitere, also known as "Hell's Gate." Whakarewarewa, situated on the city outskirts of Rotorua, is the most visited. The Maori live here between craters

*After at least 500 years of inactivity, the Tarawera volcano erupted without warning in 1886. Today, the crater attracts four-wheel tourists to take a look at some impressively bleak scenery at an altitude of 1,111 meters (3,645 feet). The small, wooden Maori churches are typical for the region – like this one in Raukokore near Eastcape (right).*

and geysers: with a height of up to 30 meters (about 100 feet), Pohuta is New Zealand's record holder. Hot water is supplied free of charge here, and used for cooking, laundry, and bathing – in various natural pools, of course. The Maori of "Whaka" make their living from tourism and supplemented the natural attractions by reconstructing a Maori fort – or pa – on a local hill.

Historically, the most significant geothermal region is definitely Waimangu, a valley situated at the foot of the dormant volcano Tarawera. In 1886, a series of eruptions, for which there had been no warning signs, left the mountain split by a massive rift. Gone were the Pink and White Terraces, formed by hot springs, which tourists had come from as far away as Europe and America to view. Lake Rotomahana – which has since reconstituted itself – evaporated in a matter of seconds. At least 153 people

died as a result of this catastrophe and three villages disappeared under a thick layer of ash. Te Wairoa, the "Pacific Pompeii" has since been partially excavated and is now one of the stops on the route through the thermal region. Further highlights include the Waimangu Cauldron, one of the world's largest with a surface area of over 4 hectares filled with bubbling water, as well as a turquoise lake surrounded by red rocks and the steaming cliffs on which it is possible, theoretically at least, to cook the trout caught at the other end of the lake.

## Round about Rotorua

The largest of all the lakes in the region is Lake Rotorua, an age-old Maori center – as the name of the local village of Ohinemutu makes clear. This village was the nucleus of what came to be the town of Rotorua and its growth was fueled by income from the hot springs. As early as 1906, the local government had a bathing house built in the middle of a local park. Today, the decorative Tudor-style building serves as an art museum. But there is no lack of thermal baths in the town over which a lightly sulfuric smell rises from the countless springs.

The Polynesian Pools are the most famous baths, but all the larger and the many smaller hotels and hostels have their own steaming pools. And some of the local citizens are liable to find themselves sitting on their very own geyser. Karen Herbert is a case in point. A geyser suddenly erupted in her garden, spouting water 12 meters (39 feet) high and spewing out great rock-like chunks of mud. Activity has continued intermittently since then,

showering the house with mud and rocks. Mrs. Herbert has since moved elsewhere.

But the hot waters with the medicinal properties that bubble up gently elsewhere from the substrata were no longer sufficient to keep Rotorua's main source of income – tourism – afloat. So the city took a look around and discovered Queenstown on South Island as an inspiring example of how best to market an area for tourism purposes. Now, this region – like its role model in the south – is a positive hive of activity tourism. The tandem-jump – a free fall from a height of about 5,000 meters (around 16,500 feet), with last-minute brakes included in the form of a parachute – provides a particularly exhilarating kind of thrill. Whitewater rafting tours through roaring currents, cross-country tours in four-wheel-drive vehicles on monstrous tires, car races in Formula 500 bolides or zorbing – these are some of the tamer alternatives. Zorbing? This attraction is native to New Zealand and involves getting in a man-sized plastic bubble and rolling down a hill.

Rotorua is also ideally situated as a good point of departure for trips to tourist attractions situated in the nearby regions such

*New Zealand's longest pier stretches into Tolaga Bay for 600 meters (around 1,970 feet) (below). The Bay and its neighboring waters are a promising destination for anglers (right).*

*Very British: Rotorua's green bowlers playing in front of the historic Bath House (large photo) – now an art museum – all in white, of course. – The Tourist Office is also located in a Tudor building (below), so the local pub, the Pig and Whistle (above right) can't be far away. Even Rotorua's kids form an orderly queue at Green Lake – just as if they were waiting for the bus in the "motherland" (below right).*

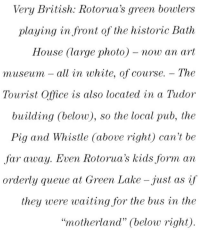

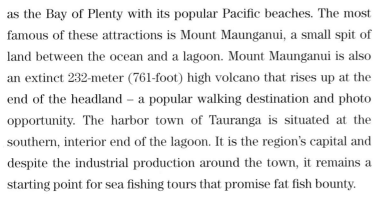

as the Bay of Plenty with its popular Pacific beaches. The most famous of these attractions is Mount Maunganui, a small spit of land between the ocean and a lagoon. Mount Maunganui is also an extinct 232-meter (761-foot) high volcano that rises up at the end of the headland – a popular walking destination and photo opportunity. The harbor town of Tauranga is situated at the southern, interior end of the lagoon. It is the region's capital and despite the industrial production around the town, it remains a starting point for sea fishing tours that promise fat fish bounty.

The Bay of Plenty is valued in New Zealand not just as a vacation center but also as a fruitful region – literally. James Cook

*Waiotapu, the "holy waters" of the Maori (above left), is the most attractive thermal area near Rotorua. One of its most famous attractions is the hot, constantly bubbling champagne pool (below left). – Not hot, just 11 meters (36 feet) high: the Haku Falls (right) are not far away and make quite a splash.*

was possibly the first to restock his supplies here with fresh fruit – leaving the area with its catchy and marketable name. Today, more kiwis are harvested here than anywhere else in the world. No wonder, then, that Te Puke is pleased to call itself the Kiwi Capital. And the New Zealanders are so proud of this success that they bestowed their own national nickname on this small brown – and now also golden – fruit. Formerly referred to as the Chinese gooseberry, the fruit was hardly known outside of gardening schools until a headmistress from New Zealand brought some seeds back home with her from a visit to her sister in a Chinese mission station on the Yangtze River. But it was years before fruit growers discovered the hairy little fruit's potential. And since the whole world now knows about the kiwi, visitors are keen to wander around the waist-high bushes and pick their own. And Te Puke is now a tourist attraction in its own right!

## Glowing underworld

This is the title claimed for itself by Waikato, the region between Auckland and Rotorua, at least for Waitomo, whose glowworm caves have been attracting visitors from all around the world since 1889. The Waikato caves developed about 30 million years ago and are structured in two levels. The main entrance is on the upper level: a dry system of catacombs and passages, lined by stalactites and stalagmites. Nature has created an acoustically perfect sound system in the so-called cathedral, where none other than the world famous opera singer Dame Kiri Te Kanawa has come to perform.

But the real attractions start 16 meters (52 feet) deeper where a river flows through the limestone. Visitors getting into the boats here will find that they still have plenty of light. But then they push off into growing darkness. And once their eyes have got used to the gloom, they'll see that the high cave roof is covered with thousands of tiny dots of light – glowworms, whose method for attracting insects is just to glow, quietly and persistently. Each glowworm has spun up to seventy sticky threads on which its hapless prey will stick. And once the glowworm feels that something has enmeshed itself in the 20-centimeter (8-inch) long threads, it winds up the victim and gets down to a hearty meal. This particular variety of glowworm can only be found in New Zealand.

*See page 66*

Mount Ruapehu (2,797 meters / 9,177 feet) in the Tongariro National Park.

# Taking the Waters

## Hot springs and warm mud baths

*It doesn't get much more natural than this: mineral residues are responsible for the colorful rim of the Champagne Pool (1). – New Zealand's hot underground is particularly active on White Island (3). – Underground forces are responsible for a number of warm, soothing springs such as Rotorua's "Polynesian Spa" (2, 4, and 5). – New Zealand also uses geothermal warmth in its power stations, where it is channeled through pipes (6). – An aerial view of White Island (7).*

Shaky Isles is what the New Zealanders call their home – situated exactly on the point where two of the earth's huge tectonic plates meet. And because these two plates – the Indo-Australian and the Pacific – are constantly rubbing up against each other, mountain ranges such as New Zealand's Alps throw up their ridges and islands start to move. Earthquakes are the result. Kiwis are used to being shaken up frequently – if only lightly – so the education process about what to do when the earth suddenly starts to move starts in elementary school.

New Zealand's geologists have placed innumerable sensors on the plate boundaries to register each and every minor tremor in the earth's crust. Unfortunately, data and statistics are not all that these scientists provide: they also serve as a warning that New Zealand is the site of a major earthquake measuring 8 or more on the Richter scale every few centuries. Seen from a historical point of view, such a major quake is long overdue.

But the plate boundaries not only constitute a set of unstable foundations: they are also responsible for the transfer of heat from the earth's interior to its surface. When this process occurs slowly and without too much pressure it can result in the formation of hot springs or blubbering mud baths – which can get just as hot. Volcanic

eruptions are the other, more dangerous side of the coin. When explosions and eruptions take place, as they did on North Island, massive mountains are the result. Rotorua benefits from the gentler variety of heat exchange and is known throughout New Zealand and beyond as a bathing spa. Long

64

Even if centuries have now passed since the last volcanic eruption on South Island, the larger island still retains the hotter springs. The best known of these are the Hanmer Springs in the hilly region of northern Canterbury. A Maori legend explains why hot water comes out of the earth here – far away from the active volcanoes: after an eruption on North Island, a piece of red-hot rock simply flew over onto South Island and raised

6

5

7

to wonder at Rotorua's attractions – and then to retire to the springs for a relaxing soak. So it's no coincidence that one of the most photographed buildings in New Zealand is Rotorua's Tudor-style bathing house.

Although the former bathing house located in Government Gardens currently houses an art and history museum, there was enough room in the extensive garden grounds for the Polynesian Spa to find a new home in a modern building. For some years now, the spa has been able to provide not only the traditional dip in various liquids but more innovative forms of treatment that include an eight-hour regeneration. The spa rooms all have lovely views over

before the first Europeans arrived, the Maori used the hot springs in Rotorua for the treatment of aches and pains – or to prevent them from occurring in the first place. That is why the mineral springs lay claim to the name of Polynesian Spa. The first tourists came in the 19th century

the lake or into the woods. For those in search of immersion in even more natural surroundings, it's not far to the warm water pools in Waikite Valley or at Kerosene Creek. The Tikitere thermal region, also known as Hell's Gate, has special warm mud bathing facilities.

the water temperature here as well. Most of the photos that advertise the benefits of New Zealand's soothing thermal baths are taken in Hanmer and show satisfied guests relaxing in lightly steaming open-air pools, surrounded by snow-topped peaks under a clear blue sky.

65

The Waitomo Cave and two further tourist caves are the property of the local Maori tribe – as are large parts of the more southerly, neighboring region of Taupo/Ruapehu. The area was probably first populated by Maori in the 14th century. According to Maori legend, their high priest climbed up a high mountain, probably Mount Ruapehu, the tallest mountain on North Island with a height of 2,796 meters (9,173 feet). Because it was so cold up above the clouds, he prayed desperately to the Gods of the mythical realm of Waikiki to send him some warming fire. The Gods

*New Zealand not only has magnificent beaches (above). Inland, the terrain makes good pasturelands. Farms such as those close to Hamilton (center right) and farmers such as the agriculturalist Te Kuti (right) make sure that export figures stay in the black.*

graciously complied and sent him fire under the sea and through the land. Since that time, Ruapehu and some of its only slightly smaller neighbors have been active volcanoes.

About 26,500 years ago, a massive eruption in this fiery region left a funnel that is now the site of Lake Taupo, the largest fresh water lake in Australasia – just one of the area's manifold tourist attractions: the mountains are popular skiing areas, the three volcano centers attract many visitors and New Zealand's longest river, the Waikato with its spectacular Huka waterfalls, is also a tourist magnet. Its popularity amongst New Zealanders and Australians alike is hardly surprising. It is less well-known beyond the fifth continent, compared with destinations such as Auckland, the Bay of Islands or Rotorua – not to mention Christchurch and the New Zealand Alps on South Island.

## From day to day

This applies to an even greater degree to Eastland, the region that juts out furthest into the Pacific. Its geographical situation and the fact that the International Date Line runs nearby along the

*Atmospheric lighting in the Waitomo Caves, famed for their glowworms, make sure that tourist revenue keeps flowing (left).*

180th line of longitude justifies the area's claim to fame as the first region to see the sun dawning on a new day. To be quite precise, the rising sun is seen first of all from the peak of the 1,752-meter (5,748-foot) high Mount Hikurangi and then from the lighthouse on the Eastcape whose own rays beam out over the ocean for 154 meters (505 feet) and can be seen from a distance of up to 35 kilometers (22 miles). Gisborne is the region's largest town and can claim to be the first city in the world to greet the sun – an uncontested and urbane title. It was only fitting that New

67

Zealand's operatic world star Kiri Te Kanawa greeted the year 2000 in a nighttime ceremony on the beach of her native town, Gisborne – a concert event that was transmitted via television to fifty-five countries. The rest of the time, however, identifying the boundary between yesterday and today is often a matter of interpretation – even without resorting to tricks such as those employed by the Kiribati. In 1999, the South Sea island state suddenly decided to move its date lines eastwards in an attempt to

profit from the million-dollar millennium business as the world's "first" state. It all came to nothing.

But where exactly do the sun's rays fall on the dawn of a new day? During the summer months in the southern hemisphere, the answer is clear: onto the Antarctic. When it comes to inhabited areas, the Chatham Islands feel that they have the edge. The group of islands belongs to New Zealand and is situated some 860 miles to the east of Christchurch, a lonely location in the middle of the Pacific. However, it is all a question of perspective. The Chatham Islands are indeed the easternmost part of New Zealand – but they are also located east of the 180th line of longitude. Yet the Chathams hold fast to their claim, and set their clocks 45 minutes ahead of those on the mainland. Back at base, however, New Zealand bases its calculations on stricter criteria than its remote outpost – the demarcation line drawn by the 180° of longitude is all that counts. Which brings us back to the point of departure. Eastcape retains its rights to the new day.

And Eastland has more to offer its guests than the right to an early start. Highway 35, which follows the coast, is an undiscovered tourist magnet, hardly known outside the country despite efforts to give it greater prominence with a new logo: "Pacific Coast Highway." The wealth of golf courses here is also a potential goldmine. There are more per capita opportunities to tee-up here than anywhere else in New Zealand. And last, but certainly not least, there is always the unparalleled opportunity to go snorkeling in the company of sharks – wearing a metal cage, of course.

A better-known fact is that the initial confrontation between Maori and Europeans took place not far from Gisborne. James Cook anchored here in 1769 and had himself rowed to terra firma. It was not a happy occasion: whether as a result of a misunderstanding or because the Maori really were planning an attack – the British feared an act of aggression and began shooting, killing several Maori. Cook had to raise anchor again. The Captain had been out in search of fresh food and water and had to leave without either – leaving only a name behind: the Bay of Poverty.

Eastland is one of the few places in New Zealand were Maori still account for about half of the population and their language can claim more than merely theoretical equal rights with English. One of the reasons for this is the Tairawhiti Polytechnic, New Zealand's leading institute of education for contemporary Maori art, presented on site in a special gallery. It's worth learning a couple of Maori words to show your appreciation: like *ka nuite pai* – very good.

*A mini United Nations: New Zealand's children come from all around the world (above and right). – Right page: 1 Here as in Australia, lifesavers are the icons of beach culture. During beach carnival, the young people show their lifesaving skills. – 2 Surfers line up before the start of a competition. – 3 When there's somebody out there drowning, you don't let a few breakers get in the way. – 4 All lifesaver teams have their own fans. – 5 Under starter's orders for a dash into the sea. – 6 When there's no motor around, muscles will get the job done.*

1

2

3

4

5

6

Morning mist over farmland on Tolaga Bay

# Haka, Hongi, and Mana

## Maori culture has long been a regular part of everyday life

*1 Once upon a time, the great Maori war canoes inspired fear. Nowadays, they are used only for ceremonial purposes. – 2 Some Maori celebrate Waitangi Day in national dress. – 3 The* marae *in Waitangi is one of the most beautiful Maori assembly houses in the country. – 4 Black-white-red: the Maori national flag. – 5 Sticking out your tongue was once supposed to instill fear into the enemy: today, it is just an expressive gesture in Maori dance. 6 Regardless of their skin color, New Zealand's kids love to practice Maori poses.*

The Polynesian peoples were some of the greatest boat-builders and sailors of all time. Setting out from Asia on their simple but eminently seaworthy outrigger canoes, they were able to colonize virtually every Pacific Island on which they landed. Around the year 1000, they began to penetrate deep into southern waters and reached New Zealand. The following centuries saw a slow decline in their navigational skills.

New Zealand's Polynesians call themselves Maori: the tribe that settled on the Chatham Islands was called Moriori. According to Maori legend, the crews in the great canoes (*waka*) on which the Maori originally set off on their travels across the sea considered themselves a unit. These later developed into the individual tribes (*iwi*). The tribes are still important, but not as significant as the extended family. In former times, the Maori lived in villages surrounded by palisades (*pa*). The center of village life was an assembly hut with especially extravagant carvings (*marae*).

The natives worshipped a large number of Gods all with different areas of responsibility (war, farming, sky, ocean etc.) Everyday life was determined by prohibitions (*tapu*) and Maori leaders were credited with spiritual powers (*mana*). Mana could be won or lost in times of war – one of the reasons why Maori history is characterized by particularly bloodthirsty tribal feuds.

Maori art consists predominantly of carving. Performing art generally takes the form of dancing. Carving skills were used mainly to personify the Gods or ancestors

5

6

4

whose effigies were often attached to the *marae* or to canoes to attract power and *mana*. The eyes of the figures were frequently inlaid with the crust of the *paua shells*. The much-valued greenstone, which belongs to the jade family, was used for stone carvings such as a stylized fishhook or a *tiki*, a

small amulet. Tattoos are applied for decorative purposes – but also to frighten off the enemy. The worldwide renaissance in tattooing has led to a renewed interest in the old Polynesian art form of *moko*.

In the absence of written material, dances and songs play a central role in Maori culture. Vigorous dance routines serve the purpose of re-enacting particular scenarios: the women tend to execute gentler set pieces whilst the men perform more lively sequences of steps. Women often celebrate *poi* dances in which they twirl small cloth balls around. The most famous male dance is the *haka*. The word once referred to all

kinds of dance: nowadays it is used to refer to a particularly aggressive combination of steps that is supposed to intimidate the enemy and involves the sticking out of tongues. The *hongi*, on the other hand, is not a dance but a much friendlier act of welcome: a Maori greeting that involves the pressing together of noses.

In 1858, the Maori agreed to appoint one king enabling them to confront the British crown as a united front. The creation of a Maori kingdom also reinforced the natives' position vis-à-vis the greedy European settlers. Today, the Maori monarchy fulfills a largely representative function. The current incumbent is female – the

sixth monarch in Maori history. About 600,000 of the roughly four million New Zealanders claim to be Maori – although scientists believe that the percentage of pure-blood Maori is dwindling. English and Maori both enjoy an official language status in New Zealand but nonetheless, the percentage of unemployed is higher here than the national average. Although some Maori have achieved wealth and repute (often via sporting successes), they tend to be found working at simple jobs – which is why nearly every government comes into office with the declared aim of raising their level of education: so far, success in this matter has remained elusive.

73

# Round about the Capital City

## There are many things worth stopping for between Taranaki and Wellington

*Art Deco figurine on the bonnet of an old-timer (above). – Panorama of Wellington: the cable car takes visitors up the hill to the Botanical Gardens (below).*

*Government buildings past and present: the classical portico of the former parliament building (above) and the new building, nicknamed "the beehive."*

Nine of ten movies shot in Japan feature Fujiyama in a role that tends, literally, to dominate the scene. This was the case in *The Last Samurai* with Tom Cruise. But not every big screen shot that seems to feature the regular volcanic cone of Japan's holy mountain against a bright blue sky was actually shot in Japan. Hollywood's budgeters discovered some time ago that given the right camera angle, Mount Egmont on New Zealand's west coast bears an uncanny resemblance to the far eastern mountain. And since New Zealand dollars go a lot further than yen when it comes to financing film productions abroad, the epic Japanese film was partially shot here, at the foot of Mount Taranaki.

Taranaki? The back and forth between British and Maori designations is particularly confusing in this part of North Island. Taranaki is the Maori name for the regular mountain cone whose 2,518 meters (8,261 feet) tower over the countryside. The region is called Taranaki – whilst the headland formed by the dormant volcano in the Tasman Sea bears the name of Cape Egmont. The National Park around the peak is also called Egmont, although the bays situated to the north and south of the peninsula are called North and South Taranaki Bight respectively.

But the region's distinctive characteristic has a further designation: "New Zealand's most climbed mountain." It seems to be a relatively simple ascent but appearances can be deceptive – especially given the sudden changes in weather conditions for which the region is known: the Taranaki area is subject to particularly heavy rainfall because the clouds tend to get caught in the slopes

Apples and more apples. Hawkes
Bay is one of the Islands' best-
known fruit-growing regions
(right). The vineyard region
around Martinborough, with many
small vineyards such as the Vynfield Estate, is not far away.

with the Pihanga volcano – who happened also to be Mount Tongariro's mistress – Taranaki was forced to flee from Tongariro's
wrath, all the way to the coast. The Maori believe that the clouds
that often shroud the mountain are tears wept for Pihanga.

Not all the areas around the mountain have such heavy rainfall. The region's largest city, New Plymouth, only has around
1,500 millimeters (59 inches) of rain per annum. The town's
50,000 inhabitants profit from the fertile volcanic earth left
behind after the last eruption, about four centuries ago. Agriculture is a booming source of income – and so is tourism. Although
the area is not very well known outside New Zealand, the Kiwis
themselves come here in droves for the wonderful beaches and
excellent surfing and windsurfing opportunities –
above all, in Oakura and Fitzroy. The coastal road
winds its way along roughly 150 kilometers
(93 miles) of shoreline and is known as the Surf
Highway. New Plymouth also enjoys the reputation of having one of the most vigorous art scenes
outside New Zealand's major cities – thanks
above all to the Gewett-Brewster Art Gallery,
which can be relied upon as a source for the latest
and not necessarily mainstream developments in
the art scene. The Puke Ariki Museum on the
other hand, is devoted to traditional Maori art. In
the mid-19th century, New Plymouth was the
scene of some grim fighting between the British
administration and the Maori over land ownership. Nonetheless, the town takes pains to present
a comprehensive view of its history. The "Heritage Walkway" inspired by historical events
includes stopping points at St. Mary's Church,

and rain themselves off. It all adds up to around 7,000 millimeters
(275 inches) of precipitation a year. Since the mountain is often
covered by cloud, it can be difficult to negotiate the fields of
loose lava or the crevices in the ice. Heavy snowfall is possible at
any time of year on the mountain itself, and it is hardly surprising
to learn that more than sixty people have died on Mount Egmont.

The symmetrical peak also holds a special spiritual significance for the Maori. Their dead leaders are buried here, at the
foot of Mount Egmont, and in times of trouble the mountain
served as a refuge, a possibility of escaping from the enemy. And
there are plenty of legends linked to Taranaki. It is said that the
former volcano was once stood alongside the other volcanoes in
Tongariro. But because the Taranaki had a secret relationship

New Zealand's oldest stone church. Its cemetery was the burial
site not only for many of the early settlers, but also for some
Maori who died during the wars, and whose bravery and combat-
iveness impressed the British commanders.

The friendly lady in the local DOC (Department of Conservation) information office has a tip for visitors: "If you have enough
time, take a drive along the Heritage Trail from Stratford to Tau-
marunui." Equipped with the pamphlet that she gave us, we took
her advice. The route takes the visitor about 150 kilometers
(93 miles) into the interior past several historic sites, ancient
Maori fortresses, former coalmines and various small museums.
The small, windy road also took us through some varied landscapes with panorama views, waterfalls and verdant pastures on

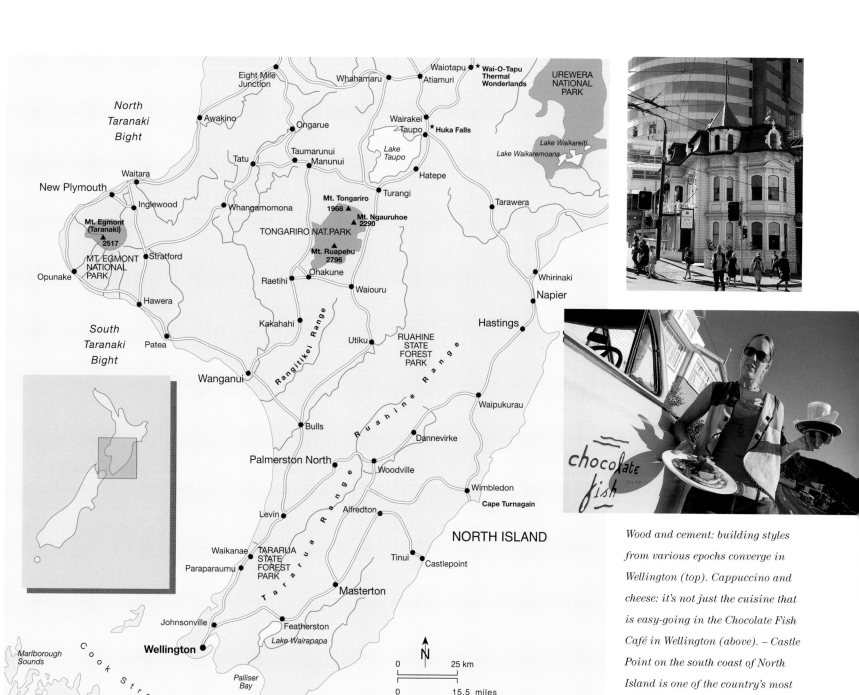

*Wood and cement: building styles from various epochs converge in Wellington (top). Cappuccino and cheese: it's not just the cuisine that is easy-going in the Chocolate Fish Café in Wellington (above). – Castle Point on the south coast of North Island is one of the country's most famous lighthouses.*

which picture-book sheep grazed quietly – a stretch of country known apparently only to the local tourists of whom we met barely a dozen during our tour on this sunny morning.

The twin region of Wanganui-Manawatu adjoins the Taranaki area to the south: like its northern neighbor, it boasts rustically bucolic landscapes whose charms have also yet to be discovered by foreign visitors. This is somewhat surprising – at least in the case of Wanganui, given that the charming valley of the Whanganui River (Maori orthography) was a popular destination 100 years ago when New Zealanders extolled its virtues as the "River Rhine of Maori Country."

77

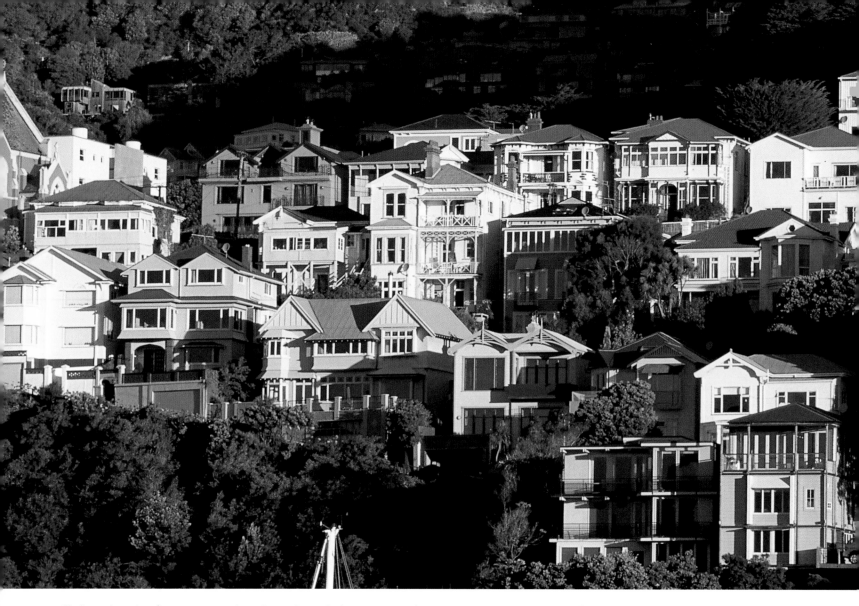

Today, the river's upper reaches have lent their name to the Whanganui National Park – an important tourist attraction, popular with hikers, and water sports enthusiasts of the quiet variety (canoes) but also and unfortunately of the louder species (jet boats). With a total length of 329 kilometers (204 miles), the Whanganui River is New Zealand's longest navigable river and was of great significance for early settlers and Maori alike, as it provided an alternative to hacking one's way through the dense forests of the interior. The long journey by canoe was difficult enough. Only the advent of paddle steamers, dismantled in England and shipped down to the fifth continent, enabled a more comfortable and more efficient form of transport and an upswing in the fortunes of small towns with large names such as Atene, Korinti, or Jerusalem.

The "Waimarie," a paddle steamer from year 1900, is anchored in the Whanganui Riverboat Centre as a reminder of this era. The waterborne beast of burden did its duty up and down river until 1952 when it sank whilst moored in the town of Wanganui. It remained under water for four decades, complete with its last load of coal, until it was raised and restored. Since then, it has been one of the principal sights in the lively 40,000

strong community on the banks of the river estuary – alongside the regional museum with its impressive collection of Maori art and Durie Hill on the other side of the bridge. Durie Hill is a little technical attraction: a small tunnel at the foot of the hill takes the visitor to the doors of an elevator. After an ascent of 65 meters (about 210 feet), passengers are disgorged onto the peak to enjoy one of the best views in the region.

Manawatu is the southern, predominantly agricultural half of the twin region. Thanks to the Manawatu Gorge it also attracts nature enthusiasts from all over the country. The path that leads through the narrow canyon takes three to four hours to walk and is only about 15 kilometers (9 miles) away from the region's biggest town, Palmerston North. Many visitors combine a trip to the gorge with a visit to the Rose Gardens in the landscaped esplanade on the banks of the Manawatu River: an international poll carried out in 2003 named them as one of the five most beautiful gardens in the world.

Visitors to New Zealand also include Palmerston North on their itinerary for one more reason: the town that is home to 70,000 inhabitants also houses the Mecca for the Kiwi's favorite sport – New Zealand's Rugby Museum. This venerable institution

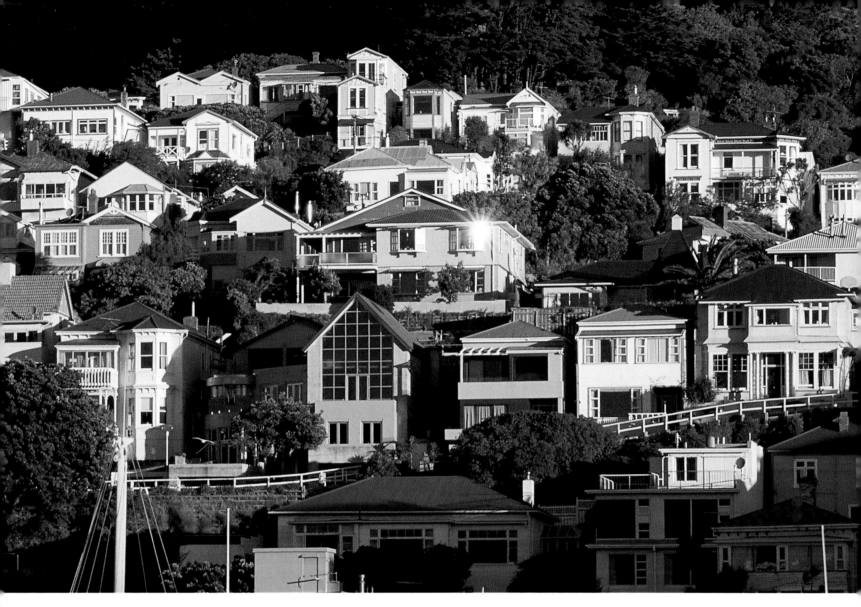

*Wellington's smart wooden architecture with a stunning view: nature has forced house-builders onto the slopes (top). – A quick break for a snack in the city center (center). Boutique with a dress by Zambesi, New Zealand's world-famous couturier (left).*

treats all aspects of the muscular team sport with the respect they deserve, from the almost devotional appreciation of the "All Blacks", New Zealand's national team, to the so-called rugby dwarves whose skills are first honed in kindergarten and elementary school. Since Palmerston North is also the site of New Zealand's second largest university, there is no lack of restaurants, music bars, and cafés.

## The land of fine wines

Whilst Wanganui and Manawatu look out westwards over the Tasman Sea, the neighboring region of Hawkes Bay orients itself more towards the east: the Pacific coast is home not only to some of North Island's most popular beaches but also to the Art Deco town of Napier and the famous gannet colonies at Cape Kidnappers. The Mission Estate Winery – the country's very first commercial vineyard – established itself here in the sun-kissed region of Hawkes Bay in 1851 (for some inexplicable reason, the bay itself is referred to only in the singular, as Hawke Bay).

Twenty-five more vineyards have since come into existence here. The Hawkes Bay Grape Growers Association has published

*Rebuilt after an earthquake, Napier became famous as a center of Art Deco architecture. Some examples worth visiting include the hall of the Rothmann Building (below) and the Telegraph Building (right).*

*Everyone gets in the spirit of the 1930s during the Art Deco weekend on the third weekend in February. Mothers with their children; the local globetrotters; a teenager with a feather boa; the photographer with a plate camera; passengers in an old-timer rally and last, but hopefully not really last, croquet enthusiasts in typical sporting attire.*

a little guide introducing visitors to all the vineyards that are open to the public. They are mainly to be found around the towns of Napier, Hastings, and Havelock North. Many have restaurants on their premises and some organize concerts and other cultural events. Most of the vineyards grow Chardonnay grapes, but since the South Island's Sauvignon Blanc began winning so many international prizes and export demand has increased, cultivation of this grape is also gaining in popularity.

A rare natural spectacle can be admired at the southern tip of this fertile bay – at least in the time between the beginning of October and the middle to end of March. During this period, several colonies of gannets come to Cape Kidnappers to nest. Normally, these birds of elegant flight patterns but somewhat clumsier demeanor when on land, hatch their broods far from human settlement on lonely islands or rocks in the sea. Here on this headland, visitors can approach these seabirds to within a few inches. Only a rope at ankle height separates the tourists busy photographing the objects of their desire from the birds themselves, dedicated long-distance fliers with a wing-span of about 2 meters (about 7 feet).

## Onwards at a leisurely pace to Wellington

To the south of Hawkes Bay, the coastal road, also known as State Highway 2, leaves its customary trajectory close to the shore and plunges deep inland. Only a few roads branch off the highway to the Pacific, providing access to Ocean Beach, Maimarama, or Kairakau Beach, which are used mainly by the locals. Most visitors only persevere southwards to take a photo of a particular local attraction: a sign proclaiming arrival at the town of Taumatawhakatangihangakoauauotamateaturipukakapi-kimaungahoronukupokaiwhenuaki-tanatahu. Standing in front of this sign, even the fuller-figured guests will find themselves slender by comparison. This version of the place name purports to be an abbreviation but it is still long enough to merit the title of the world's longest place name, far outclassing the Welsh tongue-twisters in the southwest of Great Britain who can only lay claim to the European title.

Traveling on towards Wellington, State Highway 2 runs pretty much down the center of the island and forms the backbone of the Wairarapa region. The area's name is derived from a large but almost completely unexploited lake. Indeed, tourism in this region characterized by the wildly romantic coastline around Cape

*See page 86*

Mount Taranaki, also known as Mount Egmont (2,518 meters / 8,261 feet).

# Wine-Connoisseurship as a New Way of Life

## Quality wines are big business

*1 The wine center in Martinborough offers a tasting tour through the local vines. – 2 A stop at the Highfield Estate in Blenheim. 3 Grapes ripen under nets protecting them from birds near Margrain in Martinborough. 4 Old fashioned barrel storage at the Te Mata Estate in Napier. 5 The winegrower opens a barrel on the Murdoch James vineyard in Marlborough. – 6 Tasting the wine at Mudhouse Wines in Blenheim. 7 The Vynfield Estate in Martinborough has style. – 8 It's rare to find vineyards that are situated directly on the coast such as these near Kaikoura.*

Readers of older travel guides will be told that New Zealanders belong to the world's most enthusiastic beer drinkers. That used to be true – and large amounts of the barley water continue to cross the nation's lips. Besides, beer is an important export commodity and Steinlager from New Zealand is a popular beverage in pubs and bars throughout the South Pacific.

But public attention has definitely focused increasingly on wine over the past few years. Even the smaller towns now have wine bars. Any national newspaper worth its salt features a wine column and wine-tastings have now become society events. The government is more than happy with these developments: wine is a good source of foreign currency and turnover increased more than tenfold be-

tween 1995 and 2005, from about 41 million to 435 million dollars. The area given over to the cultivation of wine grew from 7,500 to 22,500 hectares (18,500 to 55,600 acres) and the number of vineyards went from 216 in 1995 to 516 ten years later. And the boom continues apace: on average, a new vineyard opens its gates every two weeks. About 300 of these estates export their wines.

Success on the domestic as well as the international market would probably not have been possible if New Zealand's winegrowers had not invested considerable effort into improving the quality of their wines. Some slopes are now considered world-class. This applies in particular to the Sauvignon Blanc from the winegrowing area around Marlborough Sounds –

"Cloudy Bay" has found its niche on the wine menus of gourmet temples the world over. New Zealand's Chardonnays also have an excellent reputation.

In addition to the area around Marlborough on South Island, the area around Hawkes Bay on North Island, which specializes in Chardonnay, is also famous as a

5

6

7

producer of fine wines. In all, the country has a total of ten large winegrowing regions, from Northland with its subtropical temperatures, to Central Otago in the cooler south where the world's southernmost vineyard is located. This is Sam Neill's "Two Paddocks." Neill is a local actor of Hollywood repute. His partner is Hollywood director Rodger Donaldson.

The fact that New Zealand's founding fathers had a "nose" for wine – whether they were aware of it or not – is evidenced by the fact that all three of the country's major cities, Auckland, Wellington, and Christchurch, are situated in winegrowing areas. About eighty vineyards are situated around Auckland, New Zealand's only city with a population of one million. Most vineyards have tasting rooms and

8

some winegrowers take time to introduce novices to the niceties of grape differences and production techniques.

No wonder that coach tours and organized hikes to wine-tastings and vineyards now belong to the most popular tourist activities on offer in the metropolis. On the way, tour guides inform guests

about the region's early winegrowing history: settlers began cultivation in Henderson Valley, not far from Auckland, as early as 1819. The business only really got going in the 1930s when immigrants from Yugoslavia professionalized the whole production process. White wine, which is easier to grow in the comparatively cool cli-

mate, dominates production throughout the country. But in view of the worldwide increase in demand for red wine, more and more Kiwi winegrowers are branching out into this field, often with considerable success: competing for the title of best Shiraz, New Zealand came in ahead of Australia and South Africa – despite the fact that Shiraz is Australia's signature wine. Even the Sydney Morning Herald was fulsome in its praise. Applause from the rivals "down under." It doesn't get much better than this.

*They can appear quite elegant whilst airborne, but their clumsy landings have landed them with their common name: boobies (right). Gannets tend to breed in isolation, but on Cape Kidnappers they have established clearly visible colonies (below). Visitors can get pretty close to some of the nesting places (large photo). The lighthouse on Cape Palliser near Martinborough also attracts animal life: it is the site of New Zealand's largest seal colony (below right).*

Palliser is generally underdeveloped, despite the existence of a large colony of sea lions. Only local Wellingtonians drive out here for the holiday weekend. It is well worth stopping at the National Wildlife Centre in Bruce, north of Masterton on the main road. The center for New Zealand's native fauna also showcases endangered species which are otherwise increasingly difficult to find.

Masterton is the small capital city of this region. Every year, around the same time at the end of the southern summer, it makes the nation's headlines with news that is eagerly awaited even in Auckland: in the first week of March, the country's best and fastest sheepshearers compete here for the Golden Shears – the equivalent to a national championship in this discipline. After this momentous event, the town is returned to the locals. Tourists on their way to Wellington will only make a maximum of one

more stop at Greytown. For some years now, this town has enjoyed particular popularity as the home of the Greytown Hotel, reputed to be the oldest pub in the country that serves freshly brewed beer or a selection of local wine. This town was the first planned inland settlement, and today it presents well-preserved Victorian buildings and the pastel-colored little White Swan Hotel, on whose veranda time passes by most agreeably. The attractive little wine town of Martinborough is an alternative destination, somewhat further off the beaten track. Not that this is a sleepy place. On the contrary, it can get pretty lively here, in particular on the weekends when the rich and the beautiful come here from Wellington to rub shoulders and enjoy the country life. It's worthwhile making an advance reservation if you intend to visit during these peak times.

Following its curvy course, the state highway winds its way through dense forests before finally arriving at the Hutt River Valley where verdant nature has had to make way for the rapidly growing suburbs of the capital city – and have long since included Upper and Lower Hutt. This is the point at which Highways 2 and 1 merge. The increased volume of traffic and general urban sprawl has resulted in stop-and-go traffic every morning and every evening. Fortunately, Wellington does not confirm most visitors' worst expectations: despite its liveliness and its young clubbing and bistro scene, Wellington is not a Moloch. The city of 220,000 inhabitants lives up to its relaxed image – cause for caustic comments from New Zealanders on "the armies of civil servants growing fat here on our taxes." But which capital is not burdened with the weight of such accusations?

View from the Te Mata Peak (400 meters / 1,300 feet) to the coast at Hawke Bay.

# "Camera, roll ..."

## Directors on location

*1 Hobbit tours ("The Lord of the Rings") start here at Matamata. 2 "Whale Rider" was set in Wharanga. – 3 The motif of child riding on a whale is found in Maori mythology. – 4 "The Piano" was shot on Karekare Beach in northern Auckland. – 5 A scene from "Lord of the Rings" shot in front of The Remarkables mountain range near Queenstown. – 6 "Once Were Warriors": a brutal family saga about the decline of Maori culture. 7 Routeburn Forest: riverside elf forest – home to Bilbo Baggins and his fellow hobbits. – 8 Jet boat tours leave from Glenorcy and travel up the Dart River to Lord of the Rings filming locations.*

King Kong as official tender? New Zealand's dollar and Hollywood make it all possible. After director Peter Jackson, an Oscar prize winner who was born and bred in New Zealand, decided to shoot his new version of "King Kong" in his home country, the National Mint wasted no time in seizing the day: the 1-dollar coin is now a favorite with collectors and monkeys alike.

The lovesick monster was not the first cinema hero to make it onto a Kiwi coin. Jackson had previously filmed the massively successful Lord of the Rings trilogy: success that measured itself in millions – of moviegoers, DVD buyers, and quite simply in terms of net profit.

The National Bank reacted by minting whole sets of coins in gold, silver, and base metals: there was even a highly unusual 10-dollar coin issued in 2003 to provide some welcome extra revenue. The state tourist industry was no slower off the mark and immediately began organizing tours to the various film locations at which the fantasy saga had been shot – to the delight of tourists from all over the world. No wonder Air New Zealand had one of its intercontinental jets decorated with the hobbit and his friends.

New Zealand's recently acquired cinematic fame – aptly encapsulated in the country's new nick-

name "Zealywood" – came as no surprise to the experts. The islands offer an enormous variety of landscapes and countless spots of breathtaking beauty – and producing films here is far cheaper than in California. All this more than compensates for the occasionally unstable weather. And New Zealand itself looks back over a long tradition of filmmaking, which means that there are sufficient numbers of well-qualified film specialists on hand for major projects. And last but not least: the Kiwis have an excellent infrastructure.

New Zealand's very first film was produced in 1898, its first fiction

8

6

7

film in 1914. But it was only in 1977 that a film shot in New Zealand was shown in American movie houses: "Sleeping Dog" was a political thriller and it turned the film's leading actor, native New Zealander Sam Neill, into an international star. Director Roger Donaldson set his film in New Zealand.

Donaldson and director colleague Geoff Murphy, whose road movie "Goodbye Pork Pie" was also shot on native soil, proved that local movies could fill cinemas abroad as well as at home. Murphy made two further films that have entered the annals of New Zealand film history: "Utu" about the 19th century wars with the Maori and "The Quiet Earth," about three survivors of an apocalypse. Murphy received tempting offers to work in Hollywood and never worked in New Zealand again.

Jane Campion's career took a similar path. Campion scored an international success in 1993 with "The Piano," for which she received the 1994 Best Screenplay Oscar. Further Oscars were awarded for Best Actress in a Leading Role and Best Actress in a Supporting Role. 1994 also saw the production of another local film – "Once Were Warriors" – directed by Lee Tamahori, which achieved international renown.

In 2002, the Maori film "Whale Rider," based on a children's book, was a surprise success for director Niki Caro. The 13-year-old actress Keisha Castle-Hughes, who played the main character, was the youngest person ever to be nominated for an Oscar. On the other hand, the success of the seven-part film version of "The Chronicles of Narnia" came as no surprise to anyone. The first part: "The Lion, the Witch and the Wardrobe" was a box office hit. Whether the Narnia films will break the records set by the Lord of the Rings' trilogy remains to be seen, however. In 2004, part three of the trilogy "The Return of the King" was nominated in eleven categories for an Oscar. Even more astounding: the film won the coveted prize in every one of these categories.

# Englishmen, Scots, and other Kiwis

## South Island's east coast advertises its old world charms

Once the "Kaitaki" has finished crossing the Cook Straits and slowly begins winding its way through the maze of Marlborough Sounds off Whekenui Bay, the passengers begin to relax. Some are happy because the waters are more peaceful here after the rough seas in the frequently stormy Cook Straits. Others are just looking forward to this last part of the journey, known as one of the most beautiful ferry crossings in the world. The big ship, part of the Interislander fleet, glides smoothly through the quiet inlets of Queen Charlotte Sounds, flanked by islands with dense forests and countless little bays. Now and then, the cries of seabirds disturb the peace and confusion reigns at the railings whenever dolphins or seals are espied. Many a green-gilled traveler

*Some of New Zealand's best wines are produced in the winegrowing region of Blenheim, the largest in the country (above). –The lighthouse in Akaroa bears witness to a former love of ornamented architecture (right). – The combination of Christchurch's cathedral and Neil Dawson's "Metal Chalice" sculpture, made for the millennium celebrations, shows the happy coexistence of ancient and modern (right page).*

who spent the early part of the journey wishing he were back on land is sorry to see the harbor of Picton coming closer and closer.

The little town has been South Island's most important ferry harbor since 1899. Since 1962, not only cars but also railway carriages have rolled on and off here. Many tourists see the town simply as a point of transit. A pity, because Picton is an excellent point of departure for tours into the Marlborough Sounds, whether by car, on foot, in small motorboats, or in rented kayaks. The Mail Runs, which deliver parcels and post to the isolated houses that sit in the many bays along the coast, is a particular specialty. The skippers of Picton and neighboring Havelock, known for its mussel farms, are happy to take paying passengers on board. These tours are a great way of appreciating the beauty of Marlborough Sounds as well as its nautical advantages. It is no coincidence James Cook spent more than 100 days here all in all

during his three Pacific expeditions. His reports were so enthusiastic that whale catchers soon began making their way here, lured by the promise of rich bounty; Picton's museum tells the tale of this profitable era. But the town's history is also on show in the form of old ships – just as one would expect from a harbor settlement. The "Echo" is one such vessel about 100 years old that once ran a tireless ferry service across the Cook Straits, transporting goods to and fro, finally earning the ultimate accolade of Hollywood fame in 1960 as the "craziest ship in the army" under the captainship of Jack Lemmon.

Leaving the harbor and traveling southwards, the visitor will soon reach Picton's old rival, the provincial capital of Blenheim.

Since 1972, when the number of recorded hours of sunshine totaled 2,686 and set a national record, the town has called itself "Sunshine Capital." The sun's beneficial influence is much appreciated by the local wine industry. Some of the country's best wines are produced here in the Marlborough Province, New Zealand's biggest winegrowing region. The area has used its newfound fame to attract both tourists and gourmets: many vineyards organize tastings and the local restaurants have made the most of this development by serving up "fine cuisine." The Weirau Valley has even set up a 34-kilometer (21-mile) "Vineyard Tour." Frequent police controls make it advisable to rent a car with a driver – or explore the vineyards within the framework of an organized coach tour.

Highway 1 continues on its way south, running parallel to the coast. It's worthwhile following the sign to Kaikoura and driving down to the sea. Warm and cold sea currents meet here off this little peninsula, providing plenty of nourishment for many seabirds and marine mammals. Whale watching tours offer a pretty good chance to see sperm whales, orcas, and dolphins, not to mention albatrosses and other sea birds. The little town and its surroundings also have some land-bound attractions in store for the visitor – from its enchanting location at the foot of often snow-covered mountains that rise to a height of 2,600 meters (8,530 feet) to the wonderful lobsters that are tastily prepared in the local restaurants.

The highway, of which only some sections have been extended to motorway width, soon reaches the Canterbury Plains where it has to cross several wide riverbeds. In the spring, when the snow melts in the Alps that loom in the background, the normally narrow rivers can turn into rushing torrents full of rocks and boulders. Over time, this led to the development of a green plain, known by gourmets throughout the world for its tender lambs.

## Very British: Christchurch

A small range of mountains breaks the monotony of the plain and juts out into the Pacific: we've arrived at Banks Peninsula and with it, at Christchurch, the largest city on South Island. Its

Farewell Spit
Cape Farewell
*Golden Bay*
*D'URVILLE ISLAND*
*Marlborough Sounds*
Cook Strait
Abel Tasman Track
ABEL TASMAN NATIONAL PARK
*Tasman Bay*
Heaphy Track
Havelock
Picton
Renwick
**Blenheim**
Nelson
Seddon
Oparara
*Wairau*
Wharanui
Kawatiri
St. Arnaud
NELSON LAKES NATIONAL PARK
*Lake Rotoiti*
*Lake Rotoroa*
Inland Kaikoura Range
Westport
Mt.Travers 2338
Seaward Kaikoura Rang
Cape Foulwind
Charleston
Inangahua
Kaikoura
PAPAROA NATIONAL PARK
Reefton
Maruia Springs
**Hot Springs**
Pancake Rocks
Punakaiki
**Hot Springs**
Hamner Springs
Greymouth
*Lake Summer*
Cuverden
Shantytown
*Lake Brunner*
*Tasman Sea*
Hokitika
ARTHUR'S PASS NATIONAL PARK
Waipara
**Arthur's Pass 920**
*Pegasus Bay*
Ross
Southern Alps
Waddington
**Christchurch**
0   25 km
Mt. Hutt Canterbury
*BANKS PENINSULA*
0   15,5 miles
▲ 2226
Plains
Akaroa
Franz Josef Glacier
Methven
*Lake Ellesmere*
Ashburton
Mt. Tasman ▲ 3497
Fox Glacier
MT. COOK NAT. PARK
▲ 3754
WESTLAND NAT. PARK
Mt. Cook (Aorangi)
*Lake Tekapo*
Winchester
SOUTH ISLAND
Hermitage
*Mackenzieland*
*Lake Tekapo*
Lake Moeraki
*Lake Pukaki*
Timaru
*Haast*
Lake Pukaki
Cave
Haast
*Lake Ohau*
*Lake Benmore*
MT. ASPIRING NATIONAL PARK
Omarama
Pukeuri Junction
*Lake Hawea*
Mt. Aspiring ▲ 3027
Otematata
Oamaru
*Lake Wanaka*
Wanaka
Moeraki
*Milford Sound*
Milford Sound
Cromwell
1692 ▲ Mitre Peak
Queenstown
OTAGO
Taiaroa Head
*OTAGO PENINSULA*
*Lake Wakatipu*
Alexandra
**Dunedin**
Te Anau
Kingston
Dunedin
*Lake Te Anau*
Lawrence
Milton
Manapouri
Lumsden
Balclutha
*Lake Manapouri*
FJORDLAND NATIONAL PARK
*RESOLUTION I.*
Winton
Gore
Clifden
Edendale
Pahia
Invercargill
*Te Waewae Bay*
Bluff
RUAPU
*Foveaux Strait*
Halfmoon Bay (Oban)
STEWART ISLAND

Left page: The Waiau River in northern Canterbury remains an insider tip even for many Kiwis (above); not only fans of railway stations appreciate this example in Dunedin as one of the most beautiful in the world (below).
Natural forces formed the fortress-like Castle Hill (above) near Arthur's Pass high in the New Zealand Alps. Akuriri Valley in Canterbury (below).

inhabitants take pride in the town's slogan: "most British town outside Great Britain." A little exaggerated perhaps, but justifiably so – and not only because the town was founded in 1850 with the help of the Anglican Church. Visitors taking a quiet walk through the landscaped park on the banks of the River Avon or embarking up river on a flat punt will quickly feel reminded of England.

The city, with its 370,000 inhabitants, also boasts many an old building evocative of "old world charm," – even if some of these gems have been despoiled by the modern concrete constructions that also form part of the urban landscape. One such gem is the square around Christ Church Cathedral where the heart of the city beats. The decorative, neo-Gothic house of worship was built from 1864–1904. Visitors who take the trouble to climb up the bell-tower's 117 steps are rewarded with lovely views not only over the town but also over the hustle and bustle at the foot of

the cathedral. In the summer months, they might get a chance to see the city's unofficial mascot, a wizard dressed like a conjurer, who holds forth loudly and often irreverently from the steps of a ladder on all manner of matters, both secular and spiritual.

The Old Chief Post Office on Cathedral Square has tourist brochures at the ready to help visitors negotiate the inner city and visit the sights. Two hours should be set aside for this tour – not including museum visits or a cappuccino pause on Oxford Terrace. The venerable buildings include the Provincial Council buildings of 1865, the Arts Centre in the old university of 1876 and Christ's College, which still does duty as a school and parts of which date back to 1857. These buildings and the Canterbury Museum of 1870, which concentrates on history and natural history, all need time to be appreciated – and photographed.

One of the museum's most visited rooms is the Hall of Antarctic Discovery, which emphasizes the connection between

*Stewart Island, a thinly populated island deep in the south of the country, is rightly regarded as a very quiet spot (above). A Maori hiking guide for walks along the ocean shore and into the hinterland can make these excursions especially informative.*

Christchurch and the discovery of the South Pole. Preparations for many of the early expeditions were carried out right here in this town. Nowadays, New Zealand's research stations in the Antarctic are served by Christchurch airport – where the United States and Italy also maintain supply bases. It seemed logical to set up the International Antarctic Centre in close proximity to the airport. Visitors to the Centre will find information on the geology and history of the sixth continent and can try out rooms such as the climate chamber, where arctic temperatures are maintained. Guests can also go for a ride through the local scenery in the special vehicles built for use in the Antarctic. Back in the city, a memorial on the banks of the Avon is dedicated to the great British scientist and researcher, Robert Falcon Scott. Although the marine officer reached the South Pole in 1912 with his expedition, he lost the race to get there first to Roald Amundsen. Scott and his fellow participants on the expedition died on the return

*See page 102*

97

The Marlborough Sounds – one of the most beautiful stretches of coastline in New Zealand.

# The Fine Stones of Oamaru

## The attractive little town is still something of an insider tip

1

2

3

4

*1 Ralph Sherwood, the curator of the Janet Frame House, is very involved in preserving Oamaru's historic legacy. – 2 Nostalgia in the sweet shop. – 3 Two different local powers: view from the columns in front of the bank onto the Town Hall. – 4 The Criterion Hotel – a pub from the good ol' days. – 5 Sales assistants in the souvenir shops get dressed up for the Victorian Heritage Days. 6 The artist at work: Ian Andersen works with Oamaru sandstone.*

Once word had spread around New Zealand that the densely compressed, cream-colored stone around the town of Oamaru was particularly suited for the construction of elegant buildings, the local inhabitants found that they were sitting pretty – not perhaps on a gold mine, but certainly on a quarry. Oamaru stone is a simple sandstone of relatively soft consistency that is easy to take out of their earth. Stonemasons found it trouble-free to work with – a further bonus in Victorian times with its penchant for ornaments and twirls. And their clients were happy with the light-colored stone because it dried quickly in the fresh air.

Dunedin decided to use the stone for its cathedral and its town hall;

Christchurch bought the stone for its catholic cathedral and Wellington for its customs house whilst the distant Auckland had it shipped northwards for a town hall and a post office. But it was Oamaru itself that really went to town with its local building materials – especially after a further highly profitable source of income had developed just outside the town

gates. In 1882, the Totara Estate (which now houses a museum) was the first place on which lamb's meat was professionally deep-frozen for export across the sea to England. It was an important test run, the starting shot for one of New Zealand's most important and most lucrative economic activities. So the town invested in more cream-colored buildings with the

about 25 centimeters (10 inches) tall, which makes them the smallest of the seventeen species that belong to the genus. The landlocked birds with bluish feathers have chosen a spot just outside the town as their breeding grounds. Although they only waddle up from the sea under cover of dark-

6

5

result that today's Oamaru is one of the most beautiful towns in the country. Between the Town Hall and the Customs House the little network of streets around Thames Street, the Itchin, Harbour and Tyne Street presents a more or less completely preserved ensemble of Victorian architecture. The styles range from neo-Gothic to neoclassic. Some are graced with an orna-

mentation that would not be out of place on a Venetian palace. Seen in its totality, the area provides an ideal backdrop for the "Victorian Heritage Days" that Oamaru celebrates every November. For this occasion, many of Oamaru's 12,000 citizens don clothes from their great-grandmothers' era and stroll around the town, past the façades of the Courthouse, the

District Council or the Forrester Gallery. The Harbour-Tyne Historic Precinct, where most of the historic buildings are situated, is particularly busy at this time of year. Many people like to start their day at the Criterion Hotel, built in 1877, a pub straight from Queen Victoria's time.

Despite all the hustle and bustle on days such as these and the fact that it has more to offer than elegantly hewn stone, the town remains something of an insider tip, at least as far as foreign tourists are concerned. A larger-than-life penguin – made from Oamaru sandstone, of course – stands in the middle of the town. It doesn't take much for a statue of a penguin to be larger than life, given that the birds themselves, the Blue Penguins, are only

ness, the penguins seem not be bothered by the glare of headlights illuminating their progress for the benefit of the tourists. The shyer, yellow-eyed penguins, unfortunately threatened by extinction, can also be observed from a well-camouflaged bird hide.

In addition to those tourists who come for architectural and natural highlights (there is also a colony of seals nearby), the town also attracts the odd literature fan interested in the life and work of Janet Frame (1924–2004), a writer considered Nobel-Prize worthy during her lifetime. Frame grew up in Oamaru and set many of the scenes from her work in her home-town, veiling the allusion only thinly by calling the town "Waimaru.".

101

journey. The statue was made by Scott's widow, Lady Kathleen Kennet, who was one of the most famous sculptors of her time.

Two further New Zealand personalities of note are commemorated with statues on Victoria Square: Queen Victoria, after whom the square is named, and James Cook. The square is also the site of the Town Hall – a modern building, which proves that modern architecture can be pleasing, even in Christchurch. The city's biggest clock ticks away close to the Town Hall and its conference hall: it's the Floral Clock, with a face full of colorful blooms.

Another much-loved photo motif also dates back to an era before mechanization: Christchurch's Tramway. Although they had been taken out of active service quite some time ago, the

*Spectacular scenery on the Kaikoura Peninsula (above) and the special opportunities for whale watching (far right) have put the town of Kaikoura on the tourist map. – Nowadays, the whales come right into the cafés (above right). A whalebone in the garden of Fyffe House, home to the first settler, reminds visitors that these huge mammals are swimming around offshore.*

102

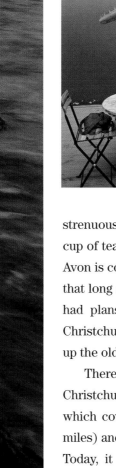

strenuous, it's always possible to escape into the Mona Vale for a cup of tea. The impressive Victorian building on the banks of the Avon is considered an architectural jewel today but it was not all that long ago – during the 1960s in fact – that the former owners had plans to tear it down. It was only when the people of Christchurch protested vociferously that the town decided to buy up the old house along with its gardens.

There are plenty of gardens and parks elsewhere in Christchurch. The most well-known of these is Hagley Park, which covers an area of about 2 square kilometers (0.8 square miles) and was laid out by the very first settlers in Christchurch. Today, it is home to a golf course, greenhouses and artificial lakes. Those in search of yet more nature should take a trip out towards Banks Peninsula. To get there, you'll need to cross the Port Hills: a somewhat arduous enterprise until 1938, when the first road was built across the hills to facilitate Christchurch's access to the harbor of Lyttleton. Today, the Port Hills are a popular excursion destination, and a cable car takes visitors to the top of the hills.

For city-slickers with something more "exotic" in mind, there is always the possibility of driving right out to the tip of the peninsula, to Akaroa. They'll find bakeries that serve baguettes, "vin rouge" on the wine menu and street signs in English and French. How come? French settlers came here in 1840 and decided to put down roots. It was not long before they began to intermarry with the English-speaking locals. Hardly anybody still speaks the language of Asterix and Voltaire in Akaroa today, but

trams were rediscovered as a nostalgic attraction and now trundle over a distance of about 3 kilometers (2 miles) through the city. Thanks to a special permit, the old-timers are even allowed to run through the pedestrian zone in New Regent Street, past the houses built in 1932 in the Spanish mission style, where the overall impression that they make in conjunction with the old buildings feels particularly authentic.

The comfortable old tramway seems part of the leisurely walking pace at which life is lived in the city center. Hectic activity is anathema here. Even the Saturday market at the Arts Centre is full of shoppers happy to take a leisurely stroll past the stands in their own good time. And for those that find even this too

*Some years ago, Christchurch's trams were taken out of the museums and put back on the streets (right). They make a good match with Christchurch's historic urban setting and typically British flair – exemplified by buildings such as the Arts Centre (large photo). – "Very British," an epithet that also applies to the punters (below right) who ferry their guests over Christchurch's River Avon in flat boats like those in the English university town of Cambridge (below).*

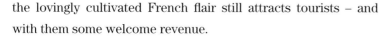

the lovingly cultivated French flair still attracts tourists – and with them some welcome revenue.

## Bye-bye Christchurch

Our rental car rolls on down State Highway 1: behind the wheel, it soon becomes clear exactly how long New Zealand's bigger island is. We stop for a break and a quick dip in the sea in Timaru, 160 kilometers (100 miles) further south. The beaches on Caroline Bay are quiet during the week, but on weekends it can seem as though South Island's entire population has congregated in Timaru – especially around Christmas, when the town celebrates a kind of beach carnival. During this time, the only spot that offers the possibility of some shade and some peace and quiet are the Botanical Gar-

dens, laid out nearly one and a half centuries ago. The gardens are home to a statue of Scotland's national poet Robert Burns – an indication that we are gradually entering a territory marked by clans and tartans. Dunedin – the most Scottish town outside Scotland, also known as the Edinburgh of the South – is not far away now. But before we get there, we take time for a quite photo stop in Moeraki, where seemingly mysterious stone spheres lie around on the beach. But scientists have long since got to the bottom of the mystery surrounding these huge marbles: about sixty million years ago, a process similar to that leading to the formation of pearls began here, as lime minerals in the sea started to accumulate around a core consisting of a fossil shell or bone fragment, sometimes even a piece of wood, ultimately resulting in boulders with a diameter of up to 4 meters (13 feet).

A distance of just under 80 kilometers (50 miles) separates these boulders from the town of Dunedin, the second largest on South Island with a population of 115,000. When Mark Twain visited Dunedin towards the end of the 19th century, he appears to have been quite delighted. The entry in his diary reads: "The people are Scots. They stopped here on their way from home to heaven because they thought they'd already arrived." It would seem that not all the inhabitants still feel this way. Some of the population has left over the course of recent years, but the visitor is hardly likely to notice this. The traditional town center, the Octagon, is still a very busy spot. Even before the first settlers sent by the Church of Scotland arrived here in 1848, this eight-sided town square had been planned. But the city fathers could only afford the construction of the two impressive buildings that flank the

1

2

3

4

5

6

Octagon after gold had been discovered in the hinterland in 1861. The Victorian Town Hall, known here as the Municipal Chambers, was built in 1880; the 47-meter (154-foot) high tower testifies to the town's self-confidence during the era when it was New Zealand's economic capital. Following a longer period of construction, the neighboring St. Paul's Cathedral was only consecrated in 1919. The third large building on the Octagon is the Public Art Gallery, whose modern architecture has been adapted to suit the style of its older neighbors. The museum features a good collection of European art but its real strength lies in the comprehensive selection of works by Miss Frances Hodgkins, New Zealand's most famous artist, who was born in Dunedin in 1870 and died in 1947.

The Town Hall architect, Robert Lawson, constructed another impressive building not far from the Octagon: the neo-Gothic First Church of the Presbyterians, considered to be his masterpiece. The Law Courts, situated in the immediate vicinity and built in 1902, are also captivating – although it suffers by comparison to the building opposite: Dunedin's majestic railway station whose tower rises to a height of 37 meters (121 feet). The station went into operation in 1904. But not only the façades of the central hall, decorated with sculptures and different colored stone, have contributed to its reputation: the impressive stairway, stained-glass windows and mosaic floors all play their role in making Dunedin's railway station one of the most beautiful in the world.

Many visitors to Dunedin like to include a day-trip to the Otago Peninsula. Although it is only 24 kilometers (15 miles) long, the headland has much to offer: a castle, two bird-hides from which to observe rare species and lovely, ever-changing views of the sea. Larnach Castle may only have been built in 1885 but it feels like an ancestral Scottish home. The castle's builder, William Larnach who was later Minister of Mines, shot himself in Wellington's Parliament building in 1898 when he found himself on the brink of financial ruin.

The Royal Albatross Centre attracts even more visitors than the castle. Worldwide, these are the only easily accessible albatross breeding grounds on which it is possible for visitors to observe the massively-winged seabirds during brooding season without disturbing them. On the very tip of the peninsula, history competes with nature in attracting visitors: this spot is home to the only canon in the world that can be fired underwater, installed in

*Dramatic contrasts: The Otaga Peninsula is known for its tranquility (below) whilst Dunedin promises a lively urban scene. Left page: Eye-catchers in Dunedin. The Octagon (1); the Public Art Gallery with its comprehensive collection of art from New Zealand (2); Frederico's Bar (3); the station attracts fans from all over the world (4), Speight's brewery (5) and Olveston House with original furnishings from 1906, which is a museum today (6).*

### Scottish tartans in the south

*Rudyard Kipling (1865–1936) wrote that South Island is populated mainly by "Scotsmen, their sheep, and devilishly strong winds." Kipling was right. The south of South Island has quite strong Scottish connections. One example is the town of Dunedin, which was initially named New Edinburgh. When the city fathers heard that numerous American towns also bore this name, they chose a Celtic designation to replace it: Dunedin is Gaelic for Edinburgh.*

*Although most of the Scotsmen who came to New Zealand emigrated from the lowlands, it did not take long for them to assume Highland habits in New Zealand: kilts, tartans, and bagpipes. Highland Games take place every year during which courageous Kiwis toss the caber. Only one aspect of their Scottish legacy is a source of dismay for Scotsmen down under: their national flower, the thistle, is considered a weed in New Zealand.*

1886 against putative attacks by Russian ships. These never materialized and now the weapon only comes up from the depths of the ocean floor for the benefit of tourists before retreating back to its bunker. The third attraction is a breeding colony of yellow-eyed penguins – the rarest species of the dapper little birds.

After Dunedin, Highway 1 leaves the coast and begins its descent towards its southern destination. But before it reaches the industrial harbor of Bluff, the road takes the visitor through Invercargill, the country's southernmost town. The city's pride and joy is Queens Park, known for its well-tended flower beds, a golf course and a small zoo. Southland Museum on the edge of the park has an art gallery and a natural history museum. But its main attraction consists of an apparatus in which Tuataras are bred – reptiles known as "living fossils." These animals, which look like giant lizards, are the last of their species to have survived a long period of evolution that dates right back to the time of the dinosaurs, about 200 million years ago. They can only be seen in New Zealand where they survived on remote islands free of predators such as rats, cats, and dogs.

The Moeraki Boulders – naturally formed spheres.

# Island of Glowing Skies

## Stewart Island attracts hikers and bird lovers

1

2

3

4

*1 Stewart Island has many beaches for those who enjoy secluded bathing. – 2 Evening colors at Paterson Inlet. – 3 Stewart Island is a popular destination for active holidaymakers, above all for kayak-paddlers and walkers. 4 Kelp is a kind of seaweed that grows like "forests" off the coast of Stewart Island. – 5 Stewart Island's tiny airport offers roundtrips by plane over the raw northern coastline. – 6 Many islets lie scattered around New Zealand's third biggest island.*

"Oh, isn't there any toilet paper here?"; "Where are the trash cans?" These are the kind of questions that tour guides regularly have to answer in the negative when they take groups around Stewart Island. Apparently, not all visitors expect to find a wilderness when they get in the plane at Bluff or take the ferry across to New Zealand's third biggest island. Visitors arriving in Oban, the only small town on Halfmoon Bay, might be forgiven for believing that they are still well within the bounds of civilization: two hotels, several bed & breakfasts, a fish-'n'-chip shop, souvenir shops, a general store and taxis for trips overland and on water. But the asphalted road ends soon after the last house has been passed and dense forest takes over. With a total surface area of just under 1,750 square kilometers (675 square miles), Stewart Island normally has fewer than 400 inhabi-

the bush trails begin their ascent. Most hikers carry binoculars in their rucksacks. The bush – as New Zealanders refer to any stretch of land that is neither town nor pasture – is home to many species of bird: 107 are listed on the island's website

6

www.stewartisland.co.nz). They include the Steward Island Brown Kiwi, an autonomous sub-species of New Zealand's national emblem. 20,000 of them are said to live here on the island although it's rare that visitors get to see any of the shy birds. But ornithologists remain undaunted and spend days camping out in the hope of catching a glimpse of their emblematic feathered friends.

Those in search of an ornithological experience without having to endure long walks though the wilderness can pay a visit to Ulva Island – an offshore islet which is home to a bird sanctuary. The return journey to Oban is guaranteed for the same day – and there is no need to worry about toilet paper.

5

tants and has a coastline that is rutted with countless bays. Most of the island is a nature reserve, accessible only via a few paths. Most visitors come here to walk – that's obvious from the large number of rucksacks that are piled up on the quayside once the ferry has landed. Most of their owners have filled them with supplies before undertaking the crossing: the goods on sale in the island's only supermarket are all a bit more expensive than on the mainland. The summer weather tends to be good in Oban, But this is no guarantee that a trip "out in the bush" will be blessed with sunshine. Thanks to a stream of warm sea water, the climate is mild even in winter, but sometimes unstable. Here, in the geographical latitudes known as the "roaring forties", strong winds are always a possibility and are often accompanied by pouring rain. The island rises to an altitude of 981 meters (3,219 feet) – high enough for many a cloud to get caught. But in the summer, there are enough warm days to satisfy most visitors.

In the winter, when not even tourists brave the stormy 20-mile Foveaux Strait ferry crossing, the locals sometimes catch a glimpse of the southern lights that streak across the night sky in a blaze of color. This phenomenon probably gave the island its Maori name: Rakiura means "land of the glowing skies." However, the Maori legends about New Zealand's creation refer to the island as Te Punga o te Waka a Maui, or "the anchor stone of Maui's canoe." The half-God Maui is said to have fished North Island out of the sea whilst using South Island as a canoe.

Today, many tourists prefer to use the small motorboats whose skippers offer their services in Oban for fishing tours or trips to the remote landing-places from which

113

# Between Sea Level and Mount Cook

## Through the remote west coast of South Island

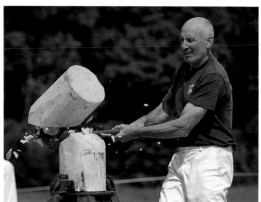

*Greenstone, a kind of New Zealand jade, is made into traditional forms of jewelry on the west coast (top). – But less artistic shows of sheer brute strength are also appreciated here such as those demonstrated during felling competitions (above). The dense forests reflected in the water on Lake Matheson are evidence that there is no shortage of wood in this region (right page).*

Deep in the south of the island, in Invercargill, Highway 1 meets Highway 6, the west coast route. But there's no coastline in sight for the time being, since Highway 6, the island's second most important road, goes up into the mountains from where it's a distance of 420 kilometers (around 260 miles) to the sea. The stretch of the main road describes a wide arc that winds its way across the country's loneliest area – the Fjordland. "Some parts of this land have probably never felt the tread of a human foot. It's just too hard to get into this mountain area," says Andrew, who has taken us hiking for a few hours along the Kepler Track. It's just a little sample hike. We'd need three or four days for the whole circular walking tour. But even this little excursion is enough to show us why so many hikers enthuse about New Zealand's southwest: deep, green mountain lakes nestle between snowy peaks and steep, jagged cliffs line the narrow fjords that cut deep swathes into the coastline. "Most of the fjords are only accessible from the sea," says Andrew. "Thank goodness! Otherwise this marvelous landscape would long since have been dotted with vacation hotels."

There is no danger of this ever happening now, since Fjordland and large parts of New Zealand's southwest are protected by their status as a National Park and UNESCO Natural World Heritage Site. Only two of the inlets are accessible by land: Milford Sound, known from countless book titles, and its equal in natural beauty, Doubtful Sound. For both these tours, it is recommended that visitors turn off Highway 6 in Lumsden in the direction of Manapouri and Te Anau. In Manapouri, it is possible to take a boat ride across the eponymous lake and travel on by bus over

*The dense rainforests come right down to the coastline at Westport (above). – The Abel Tasman National Park on the northwest coastline of South Island is suitable for swimming and kayaking (right).*

(34-mile) long Milford Track, the most popular of New Zealand's long-distance walking tracks. It is rightly considered one of the most impressive walking trails in the world – and since its popularity guarantees a steady stream of visitors during the summer months, there is little opportunity for loneliness. For those who would rather avoid the effort and the highly aggressive mosquitoes, it is also possible to get to Milford Sound by bus. Several companies offer boat cruises around the Sound or to the underwater observatory, which provides a good and informative introduction to marine fauna and flora. On sunny days, it's also worth going on a scenic flight over the magnificent panorama of mountains and lakes: some pilots even come down for a quick landing on a glacier. A return flight is also an attractive alternative to returning by bus.

the Wilmot Pass, rising to an altitude of 670 meters (about 2,200 feet). A further boat awaits passengers in Deep Cove from where a tour takes them round the second longest and deepest (421 meters / 1,381 feet) fjord, Doubtful Sound.

Te Anau, also situated on a lake bearing the same name, became famous as the point of departure for the 55-kilometer

Back on Highway 6, Queenstown is the next largest town on the route and provides a sharp contrast to the lonely landscapes in Fjordland. Its photogenic location on the shore of a long, narrow lake surrounded by snow-capped peaks has made the royal commune a much sought-after vacation destination. The main attraction is the Skyline Gondola that takes visitors up to the

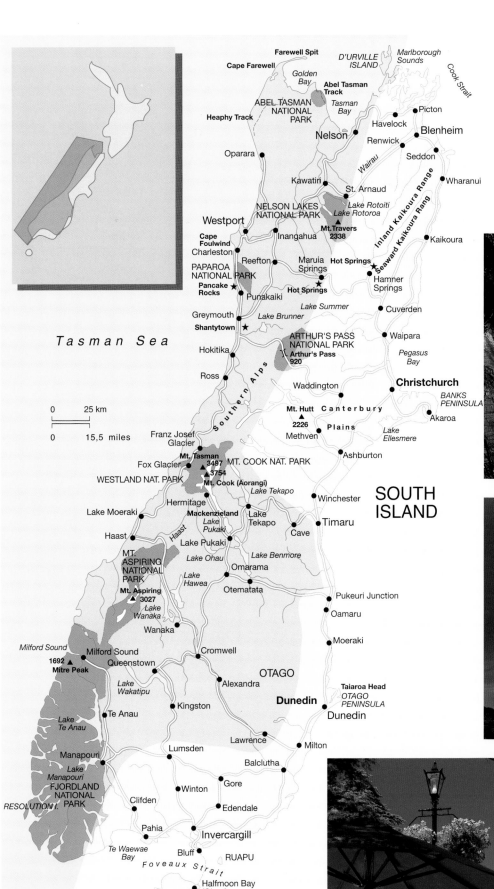

Farewell Spit
Cape Farewell
D'URVILLE ISLAND
Marlborough Sounds
Cook Strait
Golden Bay
Abel Tasman Track
ABEL TASMAN NATIONAL PARK
Tasman Bay
Heaphy Track
Picton
Havelock
Nelson
Blenheim
Oparara
Renwick
Seddon
Wairau
Kawatiri
St. Arnaud
Wharanui
Lake Rotoiti
Lake Rotoroa
Westport
NELSON LAKES NATIONAL PARK
Inland Kaikoura Range
Seaward Kaikoura Rang
Cape Foulwind
Charleston
Inangahua
Mt. Travers 2338
Kaikoura
PAPAROA NATIONAL PARK
Reefton
Maruia Springs
Hot Springs
Hamner Springs
Pancake Rocks
Hot Springs
Punakaiki
Cuverden
Lake Summer
Lake Brunner
Greymouth
Waipara
Shantytown
ARTHUR'S PASS NATIONAL PARK
Pegasus Bay
Tasman Sea
Hokitika
Arthur's Pass 920
Christchurch
Ross
Waddington
BANKS PENINSULA
Southern Alps
Canterbury
Akaroa
0    25 km
0    15,5 miles
Mt. Hutt 2226
Plains
Franz Josef Glacier
Methven
Lake Ellesmere
Ashburton
Mt. Tasman 3497
3754
MT. COOK NAT. PARK
Fox Glacier
WESTLAND NAT. PARK
Mt. Cook (Aorangi)
Lake Tekapo
Winchester
SOUTH ISLAND
Hermitage
Mackenzieland
Lake Pukaki
Lake Tekapo
Timaru
Lake Moeraki
Cave
Haast
Haast
Lake Pukaki
Lake Ohau
Lake Benmore
Omarama
MT. ASPIRING NATIONAL PARK
Lake Hawea
Otematata
Pukeuri Junction
Mt. Aspiring 3027
Lake Wanaka
Oamaru
Wanaka
Moeraki
Milford Sound
Cromwell
1692
Mitre Peak
Milford Sound
Queenstown
OTAGO
Alexandra
Dunedin
Taiaroa Head
OTAGO PENINSULA
Lake Wakatipu
Te Anau
Kingston
Dunedin
Lake Te Anau
Lawrence
Milton
Lumsden
Manapouri
Balclutha
Lake Manapouri
FJORDLAND NATIONAL PARK
Winton
Gore
RESOLUTION I.
Clifden
Edendale
Pahia
Invercargill
Te Waewae Bay
Bluff
RUAPU
Foveaux Strait
Halfmoon Bay (Oban)
STEWART ISLAND

*West coast picture book (from above): In many coastal towns such as Greymouth, the pub is still considered the most important meeting point. Lake Te Anau is the longest stretch of water on South Island with a total length of 61 kilometers (38 miles). – Awaroa Bay in Abel Tasman Park. – A freestanding flight of steps leads up to the Cathedral in Nelson.*

117

446-meter (1,463-foot) high mountain that bears the catchy name of Bob's Peak with its unique view over the town, Lake Wakatipu, and the mountains. The "TTS Earnslaw" is almost as popular: an original steamboat that dates back to 1912, it was brought here during the gold rush to provide ferry services across the lake and it is still on duty, and still powered by coal. Taking a cruise trip on the Earnslaw is a sure-fire way of finding out that the Queenstown lake is a "breathing" lake: every five minutes or so, the water surface rises and falls by up to 7 centimeters (2.8 inches).

Despite attractions such as these, the Queenstown tourist industry relies more on a category of visitor that values experience more than sightseeing. The rucksack tourists that come here were not always welcome. Nowadays, the town appreciates their will-

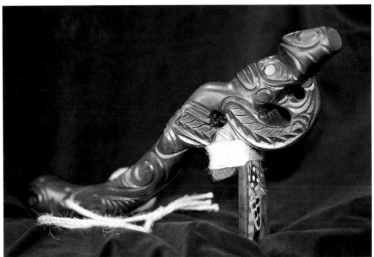

*The Pancake Rocks (large photo) owe their name to the forces of erosion that have worn away various layers of stone, leaving piles of pancakes. – Maori artists in Hokitika make sure that local greenstone is carved into traditional motifs (below left). The artful weapons of early Maori warriors often serve as a model (below) alongside traditional gestures such as the protruding tongue (left).*

ingness to pay – not for classy hotels and smart restaurants – but for the opportunity to go bungee jumping, for example. It's no coincidence that bungee jumping first became popular here or that jet-tours whiz from cove to cove between river cliffs. Queenstown has become a well-known magnet for those who enjoy activity vacations. The range of activities on offer vary from the sedately normal, such as riding and golfing, to more unusual vacation pastimes such as acrobatic flight, cross-country tours in a re-vamped school-bus on 1-meter (3-foot) monster tires, or bungee jumping off the end of a 109-meter (358-foot) long rope at a height of 400 meters (about 1,300 feet) above the town.

Back on terra firma, we leave Queenstown behind and travel onwards through the mountainous country where even the bare

---

### Wearing your art on your sleeve

*"What's fashionable in New Zealand was en vogue one year ago in London." Jibes such as these are old news: globalization has seen to it that the fashion-conscious can find the same clothes in Wellington as they would in Hamburg, Paris, and London. Better yet: New Zealand's own designers have got their own fingers in the global pie – first and foremost, Liz Findlay with her Zambesi label. New Zealand has also made a name for itself in the world of fashion avant-garde, especially in the category of "wearable art" that first hit the scene in 1987 as a gallery action in the town of Nelson. Since then, more and more artists, designers, and other creatively minded persons have pooled their resources to present their work in a show that combines artistry with music and dance. Although the show moved from Nelson to Wellington in 2005, the best designs come to Nelson, where they are exhibited in the museum.*

rocky flanks seem to provide enough nourishment for the sheep. It's worth stopping in Arrowtown, as this little town has kept the look that it developed during the days of the gold rush – apart from a few changes made for the benefit of the tourists. One and a half centuries ago in 1862, Arrowtown achieved worldwide fame when gold-diggers found 113 kilos (249 pounds) of the precious metal in the Fox River. Today, the locals concentrate their excavation work on the wallets of their happy guests.

It's not far to the next stretch of water: Lake Wanaka with a small town bearing the same name has managed to make a name for itself as a vacation destination for water sports enthusiasts and hikers in the summer, and skiers in the winter. New Zealand's third largest national park, situated around the 3,000-meter (9,850-foot) Mount Aspiring, is more or less on the doorstep.

*Okarito Lagoon is a popular photo motif because of its spectacular alpine panorama (above). In addition to such idyllic views, the west is also known for its wild coastline along which driftwood has accumulated and formed bizarre sculptures such as here in Bruce Bay (right). These wave-beaten rocks in Monro Bay emphasize the primeval nature of the landscapes.*

Referred to as "New Zealand's Matterhorn" because of its pyramid form, Mount Aspiring National Park almost directly adjoins the Fjordland National Park in the south. Together with the Mount Cook and Westland National Parks, they form part of the UNESCO Natural World Heritage Site in the southwest of the country, a protected area that covers more than 2.6 million hectares – about ten percent of the country's overall surface.

At the upper end of Lake Wanaka, the road ascends to an altitude of 563 meters (1,847 feet) where the Haast Pass – and some knowledgeable local Maori – helped pioneers negotiate the range of mountains along New Zealand's western coast in 1863. The pass also marks New Zealand's most significant weather divide: the land to the south is relatively dry whereas the area north of the pass is verdantly lush. The banks of clouds over the Tasman

*See page 126*

Two glaciers on the west coast that come down almost as far as sea level are popular destinations for ice climbers. The Fox Glacier (above) is just as easily accessible as Franz Joseph Glacier (right). Both glaciers have been receding for decades now.

# Out and About in the Land of Trampers

## Getting around on foot is the best way of getting to know the country

*Mountaineering is popular on South Island. Sometimes, hikers have to get their feet wet when crossing smaller water courses such as this one at Fox Glacier (1). Larger rivers such as those on the Hooker Valley Track near Mount Cook Village (2) have adventurous-looking hanging bridges; this track promises a fantastic view of Mount Cook (3). The Routeburn Track (4) and the Milford Track (5) will take you through rainforests. There are plenty of experienced ice-climbers clambering over Mount Cook (6).*

The New Zealand Department of Conservation calls them the "Great Walks" – eight tracks that take hikers through the wilderness plus one 145-kilometer (90-mile) long stretch of water suitable for canoeing on the River Whanganui, all well-equipped with huts, signposts, and other amenities. The tracks, of which the longest is 82 kilometers (51 miles), take visitors through some of the islands' most beautiful landscapes and are very popular, particularly between November/December and March. That is why the DOC (www.doc.govt.nz) has introduced compulsory advance booking for most of these routes –

so as to make sure that visitors find a space in the huts or on the camping grounds.

The list of these tracks include some that are mentioned in every travel guide: one is the Milford Track that takes hikers through 54 kilometers (34 miles) of New Zealand's Alps. The other two alpine tracks are nearly as popular, the Kepler Track (60 km/ 37 miles) and the Routeburn Track (32 km/20 miles). Five of the nine tracks are situated on South Island. In addition to the two specified above they include Heaphy Track in Kahurangi National Park (82 km/51 miles) and the Abel Tasman Coastal

124

the toughest around: several fields of ossified lava must be crossed. Cape Reinga Walkway (60 km/ 37 miles) along North Island's longest beach to the country's northern tip is easier to negotiate – as is Queen Charlotte Track (71 km 44 miles) on South Island. Trekking over this track is considered easy to semi-difficult. On its route through Marlborough Sound, hikers will find plenty of opportunities for accommodation and even transport for those with tired legs.

Those trekkers intending to undertake a longer tour should inform a DOC ranger before they start. Should anything happen on the way, the rangers will know where to look. Good equipment is also a must. New Zealand's travel website www.fourcorners.co.nz has put together a list of the most important items, including a sur-

4

5

6

Track (51 km/32 miles), both in the northwest of the island. Rakiura Track (29km/18 miles) on Stewart Island belongs to the favorites. Waikaremoana Walk on North Island (46 km/29 miles) leads hikers around the lake of the same name and the Tongariro Northern Circuit (41 km/25 miles)

follows a path across the inactive Tongariro volcano and round the Ngauruhoe, one of the most active volcanoes in the world. Dedicated local hikers tend to have hiked all these tracks and like to avoid them during the main summer season, preferring to stick to less trammeled routes such as the

Hump Ridge Track, in the deep south near Invercargill, opened in 2001. The track is a circuit hike of about 55 kilometers (35 miles). Alternatively, they might walk the Mount Taranaki trek on North Island. It's not just the changeable weather that has given this four-day hike its reputation as one of

vival pack containing a whistle with which to attract attention should help be needed. Hikers intending to do several tracks should purchase the "Tramping in New Zealand" guide: "tramping" is how the Kiwis refer to what the rest of the Anglo-Saxon world calls hiking.

Sea tend to get caught on the slopes of the west coast mountains and moisture is rained off. Coming down to the town of Haast, Highway 6 descends to sea level and stays there for most of the remaining stretch along the coast.

Fox Glacier and Franz Josef Glacier are the next big names on the map. Two places at which the glaciers came right down almost to the sea when the Austrian geologist Julius von Haast arrived here in 1862, the first European to explore the region. He promptly named one of the glaciers after the Hapsburg emperor back home.

Both glaciers are receding into the valley at a rate of approximately 1.5 meters (5 feet) per day and are about 13 kilometers (8 miles) long. Old photos taken a few decades ago show that they used to descend straight into the rainforest immediately off the coastline. They began drawing back about 100 years ago. Nowadays, visitors have to walk through a stretch of forest before coming to the ice masses but when they do, the spectacle is overwhelming. It's advisable to join a guided tour for a closer look at the glaciers. Walking along can be very dangerous, especially when it comes to crossing the cracks in the ice.

126

*Adventures Kiwi style.
Mountaineering in glaciers (large
photo), hiking over deep-frozen
alpine landscapes (below) or
rafting on the glacial lake of the*

*Tasman Glacier (bottom).
During the southern summer, from
October/November onwards, the
sun provides agreeable temperatures for such activities.*

A more comfortable alternative – and one that will leave your camera intact – is a walk through the woods around Lake Matheson,
the stretch of water left behind by Fox Glacier. On sunny days, the
peaks of the two mountains that rise up behind the glacier are reflected on its smooth surface: Mount Cook (Maori name: Aorangi)
and Mount Tasman. With 3,754 and 3,498 meters (12,316 and
11,476 feet) respectively, they are the highest mountains in the
country and an excellent region to explore by helicopter or a small,
twin-engine plane. The natural surroundings here on the west
coast are so impressive that the small towns that nestle up against
the range of mountains have little to offer by comparison. But
Hokitika is an attractive little settlement. It even did duty as capital
of Westland Province for a brief period during the gold rush – leaving wide streets and a few historical buildings such as the decorative clock tower as mementos of its short-lived fame. Because the
harbor is situated fairly close to some of the goldfields, the turnover
of guests and goods brought a measure of prosperity – even if the
treacherously rocky coastline also brought many a vessel to a pre-
maturely watery end. Today, Hokitika relies mainly on forestry and
its artisans – most of whom work with the local greenstone.

1

2

3

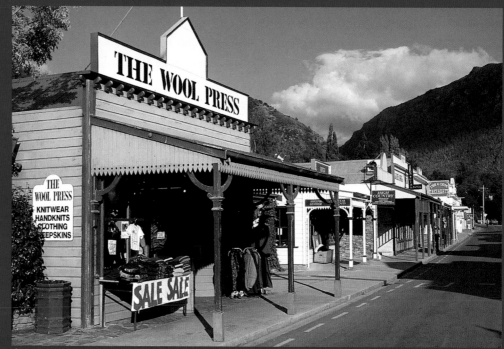

4

5

6

The stone that shimmers in many shades of green and opaque is also referred to as "New Zealand's jade" and was highly valued by the Maori. They used the hard stone (geologically speaking, there are actually two kinds of stone: Nephrite and Bowenite) not only as jewelry but also to make combat axes and tools. Many of the jewelers that work in Hokitika are descended from Maori ancestors. The stone is so hard that diamond-saws are used to carve it. Greenstone is formed under high pressure in mountain folds. It is often contained in large boulders that have been washed down-river by roaring streams. Today, the truly passionate greenstone-seeker uses helicopters to fly over mountainous areas in search of these boulders. Following an agreement signed in 1997, ownership of the west coast greenstone deposits was transferred to the local Maori tribe.

Not far from Hokitika at Kumara Junction, there is a turning off for one of the three roads that take travelers across the New Zealand Alps to the east coast. This route over Arthur's Pass is the best known and most spectacular passage. The pass was built at great cost in the middle of the 19th century but failed to bring Christchurch the anticipated gold rush profits – not least because it was still difficult for horse-drawn coaches to make the crossing. Only the railway that was constructed over the pass in 1927 simplified the whole business. Today, the asphalt road is popular with tourists. The actual distance across the Alps between Kumara Junction and Springfield on the east coast of the mountains is approximately 160 kilometers (100 miles). The highest point is Porter's Pass at an altitude of 945 meters (3,100 feet): at a height of 924 meters (3,031 feet), Arthur's Pass does not lag far behind. The route takes visitors right through the Arthur's Pass National Park, which is itself home to an extended network of hiking tracks. The park's information center is located in the small town of Arthur's Pass.

Many tourists who come to South Island with the intention of doing a complete round tour only go as far as the top of the pass (the west coast stretch is the more attractive part of the route) before going back down and rolling on along the coastline. It's not long before they arrive at the largest town on the west coast – although Greymouth in itself is not a particularly attractive destination: the concrete barriers that protect the houses from the flood waters of the Grey River are simply not picturesque, but

proved necessary. Before they were erected, the town – formerly used as a base by gold-diggers and coalminers – was subject to frequent flooding.

Many holidaymakers prefer to stop in the nearby gold-mining settlement of Shantytown, which provides plenty of attractions for young and old – including an old steam locomotive that takes

*Left page: Impressions from the holidaymakers in Queenstown. 1 Lake Wakatipu invites visitors to take a dip. – 2 View from the hillside station of the Skyline Gondola. 3 Feeding the ducks on Queenstown Pier. – 4 Nearby Arrowtown is a well kept former gold diggers' settlement. – 5 The historic steamboat TTS Earnslaw on a lake trip. – 6 A cappuccino break in Queenstown's pedestrian zone. The River Shotover is a peaceful watercourse (top) until it reaches the cliffs. – Except for stormy days, Lake Wanaka is a peaceful stretch of water whose mild microclimate is suitable for the cultivation of vines (above).*

visitors to a fully functional steam-powered sawmill. The stream in which visitors can try their luck as gold diggers is also popular, especially with children. It's surprising how often children actually get lucky, advertising their discovery with enthusiastic cries of "Gold, Gold!" Parents who pay a couple of dollars into the kitty can be sure that the owners will drop a couple of gold flakes into the water for the kids to find and take home with them.

Punakaiki is the next destination – and with it we also reach Paparoa National Park, famous for the pancake rocks that line the coast: thin slabs of stone that look like layers of pancakes. Various rock strata and the erosive strength of the waves have formed this bizarrely-shaped landscape. The sea was busy at work underground as well, hollowing out tunnels, which the water pressure forced upwards until it found an escape and burst through the rocks as fountains. Not many people know that the Paparoa National Park stretches back far into the Hinterland covering a total area of 300 square kilometers (115 square miles), some of it subtropical forest through which visitors can hike on a network of tracks. The reason for this change in temperature? The warm stream of water from Queensland, in Australia, that makes landfall here.

## Nature in all its bounty

Not far after the stone pancakes, the highway turns inland away from the coast, makes it way through the valley of the River Buller, climbing up into the mountains to an altitude of 613 meters (2,011 feet) before crossing the ridge at Hope Saddle Pass. It then meanders slowly back down to Tasman Bay on the western entrance to Cook Strait which separates the South and North Island.

Nelson is the largest town on the relatively densely populated bay (dense by comparison only to the rest of South Island). But with 45,000 inhabitants, the town still feels manageable. A stable, sunny climate, several parks, and hanging baskets full of flowers on every lamppost as well as three national parks – Tasman, Kahurangi and Nelson Lake – in the immediate vicinity help Nelson enjoy considerable popularity as a destination for holidaymakers and hikers alike.

The town was founded in 1842 and was the first city in New Zealand to be given a city charter. German immigrants also made history here when two ships with settlers from Germany arrived in 1843 and 1844. In those days, the region was shaken by politi-

*No hiker on the Milford Track can pass the Mackay Falls without getting the camera out (above). – Right page: for those who prefer boating to walking, the trip around Milford Sound provides further fantastic photo opportunities such as here at the 146-meter (479-foot) high Stirling Falls, one of several that crash down into the Sound waters.*

cal and economic difficulties because the British settlement association was more or less bankrupt. Most of the Germans settled in the hinterland behind Nelson where church services continued to be held in German until 1907. In general, however, the Germans were able to assimilate themselves quickly in their new surroundings. Today, the port city lives largely from forestry and fruit but is also proud of its growing popularity as a tourist destination. This in turn, has lured many artists to Nelson and their presence has added considerable color to the city's formerly more sleepy flair.

Christ Church Cathedral built in 1967 dominates Trafalgar Street, the main street with which it is connected via a flight of steps. The old part of the city around the place of worship features several well-preserved buildings from the Victorian era such as the almost 150-year-old workers' houses in South Street or the Tudor-style Suter Art Gallery in Bridge Street whose significance is definitely more historical than artistic.

The Botanical Reserve is the city's most beautiful park. Situated on a hill, its location affords beautiful views across the town and over the bay of Nelson Haven. A monument erected in the middle of the park marks "The Centre of New Zealand" – a proud claim that is not necessarily geographically accurate. It just happens to be the spot at which surveyors started measuring the Nelson region in 1877. But the park is also a little pilgrimage

site for enthusiastic rugby fans. One of the playing fields was the site where New Zealand's favorite game was first played in 1870.

Even before the arrival of the settlers, the region around Nelson played an important role. When the Dutch navigator Abel Tasman turned up here with two ships on New Zealand's west coast in 1642 – the first European to have come this far – he anchored not far from today's Nelson. Local Maori launched an attack on the European sailors, resulting in four fatalities. Tasman raised anchor, prepared for departure and named the cove "Murderer's Bay." The somewhat negative designation has now been replaced with the name Golden Bay. On the seaward side of the bay, sea currents have created a narrow, 25-kilometer (16-mile) long sand headland, the Farewell Spit. Since numerous seabirds use the dunes as a stop-over and also for brooding and nesting, the "Finger in the Sea," as it is called, has been declared a nature reserve and is off-limits to tourists. Just a few tour operators have been given special licenses to drive to the northernmost tip of South Island on four-wheel drives and are allowed to take visitors through this fascinating habitat.

Leaving Golden Bay and Nelson behind and traveling eastwards, visitors only have another 150 kilometers (93 miles) to travel before arriving back in Picton where a sigh of satisfaction marks the end of a wonderful round-trip around South Island.

The nearly perfect pyramid form of Mount Aspiring rises to a height of 3,030 meters (9,941 feet).

# Sweet Dreams, Castle Ghost!

## From luxury hotels to hostels – there's plenty of choice

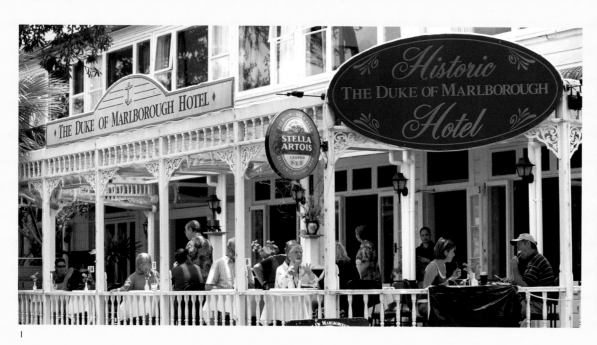

*1 Victorian ambiance in Russell: the Duke of Marlborough Hotel.*
*2 This garden would grace any castle: Taupo Lodge in Taupo.*
*3 Less auspiciously comfortable: the bed & breakfast charm of La Belle Villa in Akaroa. – 4 The Puka Park Lodge on Coromandel Peninsula is reminiscent of an English club. – 5 One-and-a-half centuries of hospitality under its belt: The Cardrona Hotel near Wanaka.*
*6 New Zealand's only real castle: Larnach Castle on Otago Peninsula.*

New Zealand's hotels are a good indication of how much the country has changed – mostly for the good! Naturally, the country always had its fair share of hotels designed to accommodate the British Empire's nobility. But it was badly prepared for the onrush of visitors from around the world who came here in the wake of a tourist boom expecting a certain level of comfort. However, the government was quick to recognize tourism's economic potential and had hotels built and operated in strategically selected places. And although these were not luxury establishments, they made it quite clear to the local hostel operators that as

from now, an en-suite bathroom was standard.

All that is history now and international hotel chains have long understood that New Zealand consists of more than just Auckland. Big hotel names are represented in all the major and most of the smaller towns that have proved attractive to tourists.

Happily, modernization and globalization is just one aspect of New Zealand's hotel industry. The other is the provision of luxury. More and more hotel owners have succeeded in acquiring reputations as establishments of superior standing. One example is the couple who own Lake Taupo

Lodge, a hotel that has garnered international praise and several stars. The Puka Park Resort on Coromandel Peninsula, which is managed by one of the largest hotel enterprises in the world, enjoys a similarly prestigious repute.

The third trend in New Zealand's hotel trade takes the visitor to the

136

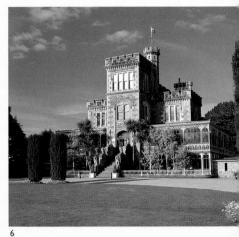

6

4

5

other end of the market. Inexpensive lodgings for backpacker tourists have sprung up in New Zealand like mushrooms after warm rain. There is no shortage of clients, since Kiwi land is a constant favorite amongst rucksack travelers. Nonetheless, even this prolific branch of hostelry has witnessed an improvement in standards: six-bed rooms with all the charm of a barrack's dorm have been replaced by two-bed chambers, modern bathrooms and even internet connections.

The fourth trend is the most visually pleasing; traditional hotels are being restored, representative old buildings transformed into up-

market inns, whilst old villas are getting a new lease of life as superior boutique hotels. La Belle Villa in Akaroa is an example of one such conversion. The smart lodge that welcomes visitors with a fire burning in the hearth once housed a doctor's surgery.

Representation was the primary objective behind the building of Larnach Castle in 1871, when its construction was commissioned by a rich businessman and politician. Today, New Zealand's "only castle" is a tourist attraction. Having come this far, the owners feel that visitors should be encouraged to stay overnight. Guests cannot actually lay their weary

heads on pillows in the main house, but the former stables have been converted into comfortable lodgings. Whether the castle ghost invoked by Larnach Castle's website actually finds its way from the ancestral home to the neighboring sleeping quarters is something that guests will have to find out for themselves.

Cardrona Hotel was originally built in 1863 during the gold rush. A renovation financed by a more contemporary form of investment has brought the building up to date with modern accommodation standards. Its 16 rooms are often fully booked, above all in winter when the neighboring ski-lifts are running.

The Duke of Marlborough Hotel, a white mansion in New Zealand's first capital city Russell, is a further example of many that testifies to this kind of traditional hospitality. And last but not least, no account of the hotel business in New Zealand would be complete without a mention of the many bed & breakfasts, which finance the expensive maintenance of their Victorian premises by taking in paying guests.

# Planning, Traveling, Enjoying

## Accommodation

In New Zealand, the designation "hotel" does not always mean that travelers will find a bed on which to rest their aching limbs. What they will always find is a refreshing beer. In rural areas, pubs often used to double up as hotels, but the two or three rooms that they once set aside for visitors have long since been turned into

*Keep on trucking! With or without roadworks, the open road beckons in New Zealand.*

Motels are used primarily by drivers, for whom they provide simple, cheap accommodation with parking spaces directly in front of the rooms. Hostels are aimed at backpackers of all ages and are very inexpensive, owing to their great number and the resulting competition for customers. Sometimes, visitors must make do with a bed in a small dormito-

ry whilst others have single rooms and accommodation for couples. In addition to the private operators, the New Zealand Youth Hostel Organization is also very popular with low-budget travelers.

Self-catering apartments have also gained in popularity and may be rented in all towns and in some of the smaller places that are popular as tourist attractions. The "farmstays" that offer guests the chance to stay overnight in a particularly rural environment are a specialty in New Zealand, although "farm" does not necessarily refer to active farming. Some of these establishments now concentrate exclusively on tourism and have only kept a few animals to pet or to ride. An overview of these lodgings can be found under www.newzealand.com.

*A first-class sample of the 15,134 kilometers (9,404 miles) of coastline.*

storerooms. In the towns, however, most hotels always provide the accommodation associated with the term – with rooms that range from the simple to the luxurious. Private homes with only a few guest rooms tend to refer to themselves as a "homestay" or a

bed & breakfast. Breakfast in these cases is cooked, and includes eggs, bacon, and similar high-calorie foodstuffs. By contrast, the much vaunted "free breakfast" offered by middle class hotels is generally limited to orange juice, coffee, and donuts.

*Doing things in style: a tour of Napiers' Art Deco district.*

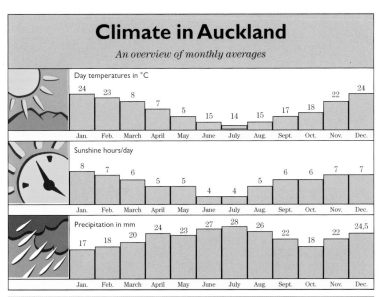

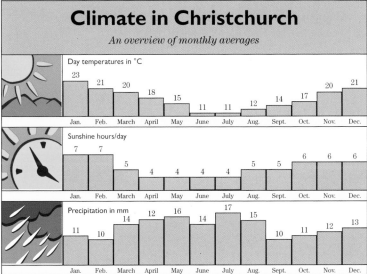

*Art can take many forms: two dapper participants at the Wellington Arts festival.*

## Arrival and departure

The plane journey from London takes about 25 hours, including a stop-over in Asia. Flight times from New York total about 19 hours and 12.5 hours from Los Angeles. Visitors must be in possession of a passport that still has at least three months' validity at the time of their planned departure. Tourists not intending to stay for longer than three months do not normally require a visa. Different regulations apply to visitors from certain countries.

Tourists are not allowed to work in New Zealand, not even in small, part-time jobs. However, there is a special program for young people (aged 18-30) that allows them to finance a longer vacation by working. They can apply for a 12-month visa within the framework of the "Working Holiday Scheme." Information is provided on the Embassy website under www.nzembassy.com.

At the moment, those departing from New Zealand currently have to pay a "departure tax" of 25 Dollars. It must be paid at the airport.

## Before you leave

Special vaccinations are normally not necessary. Important, personal medication should be packed in carry-on hand luggage, just in case there is a problem with delayed or lost luggage.

## Climate/ When to travel

Since New Zealand is situated in the southern hemisphere, the seasons are the "reverse" of those in Europe and North America. The warmest months are November through February, the coolest are those from June to August, which also constitute the skiing season. Temperatures can vary considerably throughout the country: the north is subtropical whilst the south is often influenced by Antarctic winds. Summer temperatures in Auckland often exceed 30 degrees Celsius and seldom fall below 10 degrees in the winter. Christchurch has been known to experience similar temperatures in the summer but the average is closer to 25 degrees. In the winter, they lie between 5 degrees above

*No manners? A yawning seal gives visitors that special view.*

1

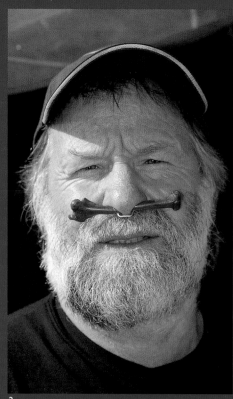

2

3

4

5

6

and 8 degrees below freezing. New Zealand has a typically maritime climate with a mild, rainy climate. The weather is extremely changeable.

The best time to visit New Zealand is in the summer months although it is worth remembering that most Kiwis tend to travel themselves during the main vacation season (mid December to the end of January/mid February). It's as well to make advance reservations for accommodation and vehicle rental during these peak vacation times. Many attractions will be overcrowded and prices are higher. It's preferable to travel in spring (October/November) or fall (March/April). It can be surprisingly cool in spring-time and snow is widespread in higher altitudes.

## Currency

The New Zealand dollar consists of 100 cents. Coins are available in denominations of 5, 10, 20, and 50 cents as well as 1 or 2 dollar coins. The flip side of the smallest coin shows a Tuatara, the only surviving animal regarded as a contemporary of dinosaurs, which lives in New Zealand. Bank notes

*The Wildfoods Festival in Hokitika takes its name seriously: the Stone Age Family Flintstone requests the pleasure of your company. – 2 Bone recycling. – 3 Skinned – and then made into possum meatballs. If you're curious about what you're eating, you can check out the fur. – 4 A delicacy: toasted grasshoppers. – 5 Caterpillar, anyone? – 6 Best not to ask what's in the plastic bags.*

are issued with a value of 5, 10, 20, 50, and 100 dollars. They are no longer made of paper but from a special kind of plastic compound which makes them more durable and more difficult to forge. Sir Edmund Hillary is featured on the 5-dollar note as a young man around the time that he became the first man to climb Mount Everest.

*No bluff in Bluff. All the distances on this signpost have been carefully calculated.*

## Customs

New Zealand exercises strict controls at all points of entry into the country to check for food, feathers or any other products that could introduce pests or other agents harmful to its agriculture. Even an apple in

*Scorching Bay near Wellington is ideal for swimming and scuba diving.*

your hand luggage will be prosecuted with an on-the-spot fine. Specially trained sniffer-dogs soon find the culprits. Tourists entering the country are permitted to bring 1.25 liters of alcoholic spirits, 4.5 liters of wine or beer, 200 cigarettes per person and presents with a maximum value of 700 dollars. These restrictions are subject to change and it's worth checking the customs website before you leave under www.customs.govt.nz.

Medications that might also pass as drugs should be accompanied by special doctor-issued certification, in English if possible.

## Electricity

Voltage in New Zealand lies between 230 and 240 volts. Power outlets accept flat three- or two-pin plugs for which all foreign travelers will need adaptors. Travelers from the United States may find that they also need power transformers (from 120 to 220–240 volts), unless their electronic devices have multi-volt options (many mobile phones and laptops integrate this facility in the plug).

Hotel bathrooms have power outlets for two-point shaver plugs.

*A burst of color: pottery in Nelson.*

# Festivals/ National holidays

The traditional festive season has now been extended to include the increasingly popular food and wine festivals, most of which take place during the warm summer weeks when most tourists can be expected. Cultural festivals in the cities are also scheduled for the winter months. The most important holidays are:

January 1/2: New Year;
February 6: Waitangi Day;
March/April: Good Friday and Easter; April 25: Anzac Day;
1st Monday in June: Queen's birthday;
4th Monday in October: Labor Da;
December 25: Christmas Day;
December 26: Boxing Day.

In addition, there are some holidays that are only celebrated at regional level. Many national holidays that occur on weekdays are deferred and taken as part of a long weekend.

*Invitation to cool down on a hot day in East Cape.*

# Handicapped travel

Modern public buildings or those that have been comprehensively renovated are required by law to provide handicapped access. Many hotels, restaurants, railway stations, airports, and shopping centers have also been modified to provide wheelchair access – as have many movie theaters, theaters, and other tourist attractions. Some car hire companies will provide wheelchair-compatible cars if given sufficient notice.

*In the Botanical Gardens of Wellington.*

# Health

Thromboses are a health hazard on long flights unless passengers take care to move around. Visitors traveling in cramped tourist class conditions should follow the stretching exercise instructions supplied by all airlines – all of which can also be carried out in a seated position. It is better to get up periodically and walk up and down the aisles.

*All of a kind: sand waves at Cape Farewell.*

# Wellington

## The best walking tour around the city's sights

"Well done, Wellington." Praise from an Australian magazine for the new layout of Wellington's harbor parade is praise indeed – coming from the archrival. But the new walkway from the Bay over to the Te Papa National Museum is really something special. Visitors should set aside a whole day if they want to do justice to the Te Papa Museum, with its Maori artifacts and natural history collection. If you fancy a stroll across to Queens Wharf, you might also consider going round the Museum of Wellington City & Sea.

Our tour takes us down Grey Street to Lambton Quay. Although it is now situated at some distance from the sea, this quay once marked the harbor line. Wellington has always been locked in battle with the sea when it came to providing land for its growing community, since expansion into the hinterland was restricted by the local hills – although these have also long been built upon: the historic cable car was constructed here as early as 1902. Today, it does duty as a tourist attraction whose hill station affords an impressive view over Wellington. It's possible to walk back down into town through the Botanical Gardens. But if you only have one day, it's better to take the cable car back down and turn left onto Lambton Quay, the main shopping street. Those who prefer to keep their hands in their pockets should at least take a quick look in Kirkcaldie & Stains, "Wellington's answer to Harrods of London." Although this is a slight exaggeration, the store, which first opened its doors in 1863, remains an impressive institution. Moving on, we find that the hustle and bustle of boutique shopping is gradually giving way to the quieter pace of life in the government district – Wellington has been the country's capital (and the southernmost capital in the world) since 1865. Its status is symbolized by the Beehive, the appropriately nicknamed parliament and government building opened in 1980 after an eleven-year construction period. The modern building is flanked by the older neo-Gothic

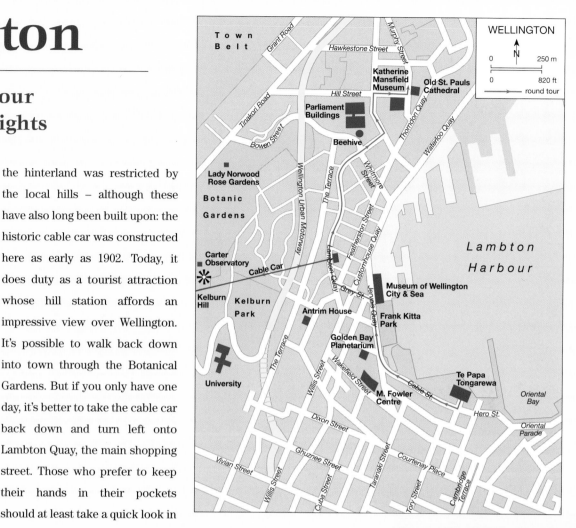

*Wellington modern: the Te Papa National Museum.*

Parliament Building. The Government Buildings situated opposite have also found a new function: nowadays, students of law at Wellington University can boast premises in the second largest wooden building in the world (after a Japanese temple). One of the city's oldest districts, Thorndon, is situated to the north of the government area. Its most famous attraction is the former cathedral of Old St. Paul's which is now used for concerts, weddings, and similar events. Thorndon's second most popular attraction is the birthplace of New Zealand's most famous novelist, Katherine Mansfield, situated a little further away. Looking for something really spe-

*Historic: St. Paul's Church.*

cial to finish your tour? The National Tattoo Museum in Abel Smith Street (it's a good idea to take a taxi) shows how the most popular tattoos favored by sailors of old – and more recently by European and American youth – derive from patterns based on historic Polynesian symbols.

Special antithrombosis stockings are also helpful.

A tried and tested antidote for jet-lag caused by the time difference after long distance flights is a large helping of natural daylight.

Nonetheless, most people take a few days to adjust to the new time zone and should avoid all too strenuous activities during this time. From a medical point of view, New Zealand is considered a

*Small aircraft can land on the glaciers on Mount Cook.*

### Full steam ahead into your vacation

*"All aboooaard!" is what you'll hear twice a day from October to April when New Zealand's last regularly operated steam locomotive chugs off from Kingston on Lake Wakatipu. The "Kingston Flyer" takes about forty minutes to cover the 14 kilometers (9 miles) to its destination, the town of Fairlight. The seven carriages, which date back to the year 1898, are also attached to the locomotive: on cold days, the steam is a welcome source of heat for shivering passengers. Now and then, steam locomotives also roll along other tracks such as the TranzAlpine-Route in the Alps or on the Taieri-Gorge-Route near Dunedin. Private railway fans who are members of the Main Line Steam Trust rent these locomotives for trips that can last for hours, or days, depending on the destination. The Trust's eleven steam-powered veterans are stationed in Auckland, Wellington, and Christchurch; www.mainlinesteam.co.nz provides information on trips down memory lane.*

*On the Driving Creek Railway near Coromandel Town.*

safe country. The network of hospitals and other medical institutions is fairly dense and the standard of medical care is high. Hygiene is also of a high standard and tap water can be drunk everywhere. Since ultra-violet radiation from the sun's rays is particularly

high in New Zealand (the country has one of world's highest skin cancer rates), it is advisable to cover exposed areas with sunscreen and protective clothing.

Hikers are advised to drink water from rivers and lakes only after it has been boiled or filtered since it

*Appetizers in Fleur's Place, Moeraki.*

can contain bacteria that cause diarrhea. Medical treatment in New Zealand is not generally covered by European insurance schemes so it is recommended that visitors take out special travel insurance for the duration of their stay.

## Information

The generally excellent tourist infrastructure in New Zealand includes the extensive network of information offices. Most of them are signposted as an "i-site," but there are also some smaller information offices, some of whom are managed by tour operators using them to promote and sell their own products and programs.

The "i-sites" are nearly always well equipped with brochures, many of which are more informative than tourist information provided in other countries. Staff at the "i-sites" tend to be very well informed and extremely helpful, especially in those centers that lie off the beaten track. New Zealand's official tourist website

www.newzealand.com is an excellent source of information, not only for those preparing their journey at home but also for those already on the road. The New Zealand Tourist Bureau in Great Britain (New Zealand House, Haymarket, London SW1Y 4TQ, tel.: 00 44/20 79 30 16 62) provides information on tourist activities. Tourism New Zealand also maintains its own hotline round the clock.

## Museums

New Zealanders enjoy collecting. So there are plenty of collections on view in New Zealand: from hotchpotch assortments of grandma's household goods to the comprehensive assembly of objects that constitute New Zealand's

National Te Papa Museum in the capital Wellington. The museum website under www.nzmuseums.co.nz covers nearly all of New Zealand's museums and is divided into twelve subcategories. Even areas of specialized interest, such as maritime museums, list close to fifty addresses.

## Postal services/ Internet

Normal post office opening hours are Monday to Friday from 8.30 a.m. to 5 p.m. Smaller post offices often remain closed on Saturdays, only the larger branches open between 9.30 a.m. and 1 p.m. The New Zealand Post Office has opened many smaller offices on the premises of other shops and these

145

so-called post-shops stay open for as long as their hosts. Central post offices will accept letters *poste restante* if the designation is specified next to the name of the addressee on the envelope, followed by the address of the Central Post Office in the respective town. New Zealand's postboxes are generally emptied once a day around 5 p.m. Additional collections take place in city centers around midday.

There are internet cafés throughout New Zealand, but only the establishments in larger cities usually provide sufficient terminals and a rapid broadband connection. Most backpacker accommodations have computers with internet connections, as do many hotels (often an expensive service). Public libraries only let tourists use their internet service if local members happen not to be using it.

## Safety

New Zealand is regarded as one of the safest countries in the world. In rural areas car owners often leave their vehicles unlocked. But criminality is moderately prevalent in the larger cities, especially when linked to drug abuse. It is advisable to take the usual precautionary measures: do not go out at night carrying large amounts of cash or wearing showy jewelry. Make sure that money and personal documents are inaccessible to pickpockets. If the worst does come to the worst: the New Zealand police are reliably helpful.

## Shopping

The quality and quantity of shopping opportunities has improved with the country's increased prosperity and the growth in international tourism. However, many shops still close in the early evening: opening hours from Monday to Friday are from 9 a.m. to 5.30 p.m. In the main cities, shops tend to stay open longer on Thursdays or Fridays (until 9 p.m.). On Saturdays, shops open until 12.30, or 5 p.m. in the larger cities. There is a general trend towards longer opening hours in the urban centers. This already applies to supermarkets of all sizes and for the "Dairies" (corner shops), which are also open on Sundays. Shopping centers in the cities tend to open around midday on Sundays.

Banks are normally open from 9.30 a.m. to 4.30 p.m. However, New Zealand dollars can also be drawn at any of the numerous cash dispensers or ATMs using foreign bank cards and a PIN.

Credit cards are widely used in New Zealand, even when it comes to paying smaller amounts. All prices include a "Goods and Services Tax" (GST – a kind of value added tax) which is not re-funded to tourists and foreigners at the point of exit, contrary to practice in other countries.

Leading stores are Smith and Caughey in Auckland, Kircaldie and Stains in Wellington, Ballantynes in Christchurch, and Arthur Barnett in Dunedin. All of them provide a comprehensive service. Markets

*A birds-eye perspective: view of the three lakes from Rotorua.*

are generally given over to the sale of arts and crafts products. The Victoria Park Market in Auckland is open daily, the Wakefield Market in Wellington is open from Friday to Sunday and on holidays, and the stalls at the Arts Centre Market in Christchurch are also open at the weekends.

In addition to the usual souvenirs, popular mementos from New Zealand are textiles from New Zealand's up-and-coming designer studios or wool products – hardly surprising, given an indigenous

*Wine tasting: testing the bouquet.*

sheep population that goes into millions. Carvings and other handicrafts produced by Maori are also popular. Since there are already quite a few forgeries around, it's worth looking out for the *toi iho* Maori trademark (although not all Maori artisans are members of this association) or buying products – especially the expensive pieces – from specialist galleries. The same applies to the costly paua or greenstone jewelry.

Sheepskin products are available at most of the places frequented by tourists. They generally take the form of slippers, mittens, and whole sheepskins. The latter tend to prove problematic when it comes to packing for the return flight since they are bulky and also relatively heavy. Foodstuffs are also increasingly popular as souvenirs – including local cheese specialties (tightly wrapped to avoid leaking smells) and sweets made with kiwis or honey. Marmite is a more eccentric but very typical memento: it's a healthy, vegetarian sandwich spread with an intense, yeasty taste made from residues left over during the brewing process. The thick, brown, paste was first made in Great Britain but is regarded by many in New Zealand as a counterpart to the similarly concocted Australian icon product, Vegemite.

# Size, location, topography

With a surface area of about 270,000 square kilometers (105,000 square miles), New Zealand is slightly larger than the

*Fisher's luck: a freshly-caught trout in Turangi.*

"mother country", Great Britain. Of these, 150,000 square kilometers (58,000 square miles) are occupied by South Island, about 114,000 (44,000 square miles) are taken up by North Island, and the rest is distributed over various smaller islands, of which Stewart Island is the largest. The coastline covers an overall distance of 15,134 kilometers (9,404 miles). Going from north to south, the

*See page 152*

# Discovering New Zealand

## The five most beautiful routes

### 1. Auckland – Bay of Islands – Cape Reinga – Waipoua Kauri Forest – Auckland (approx. 1,000 kilometers / 620 miles)

The journey starts spectacularly as we cross Auckland's symbolic landmark, Harbour Bridge. For most of this roundtrip, we'll be following the signs marking New Zealand's State Highway 1 that connects the southern part of South Island with the northernmost tip of North Island, Cape Reinga. This is our destination but for the time being, we take our first break in the Town Basin of Whangarei with its small harbor, cafés and restaurants.

The Bay of Islands deserves at least one overnight stay. The large inlet dotted with islands not only boasts wonderful scenery but also numerous historic landmarks. Once we've seen the last of these at the lighthouse, high above the point where the Tasman Sea and Pacific Ocean meet, our direction changes and we head back towards Auckland – taking a detour via State Highway 12 to admire the Kauri trees in Waipoua Kauri Forest.

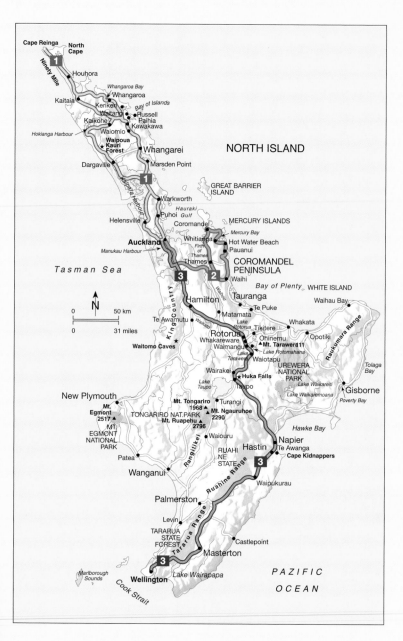

*Photo caption: The lighthouse on Cape Reinga is – almost – New Zealand's northernmost point.*

### 2. Coromandel Peninsula (about 430 kilometers / 270 miles)

Although the town of Thames, known as the "Gate to Coromandel," is only about 115 kilometers (70 miles) from Auckland, visitors planning a roundtrip over the mountainous peninsula should calculate at least two days for the trip. Highway 25 takes you round the lower part of the elongated peninsula. A short detour near Coromandel Town, the old gold digging settlement, will give you a chance to take a tour through wildly impressive scenery on the old narrow gauge Driving Creek Railway.

Once the road has crossed the peninsula, it provides access to some of the best beaches on the Pacific Ocean, including Hot Water Beach, on which you can dig your own "bathtubs" in the sand and see them fill up with hot ground water. Because of its strong currents, the beach is not really suitable for swimming.

Highway 25 turns off towards the south near Hikuai. If you turn right here, the road will take you over the peninsula ridge, back to Auckland.

## 3. Auckland – Rotorua – Lake Taupo – Napier – Wellington (about 800 kilometers / 500 miles)

This trip straight down North Island will give you the opportunity of viewing many of the island's major sights. English tourists came to Rotorua as early as the 19th century to witness the famous volcanic scenery. Hot mud springs, geysers and steaming lakes can all be visited with a minimum of discomfort –

*Camper's picnic break on the Bay of Plenty.*

and followed by a visit to the spa that is guaranteed to sooth body and soul.

Lake Taupo attracts not only trout fishers from all over the world: it

is also a good point of departure for tours into the 2,000-meter (6,560-foot) high volcanic region – the very heart of New Zealand's North Island. Highway 5 takes the

visitor back out of the mountains and down to Napier, a town on the Pacific that was completely devastated by an earthquake in 1931 and rebuilt in the Art Deco style. As a result of this massive quirk of nature, the town is now a premier tourist attraction.

The road only seems to come to an end in the Bay of Wellington, the country's capital. Once we've taken the ferry across Cook Strait, we'll find the signs for Highways 1 and 5 waiting for us again. But let's cross that Strait first.

*Cliffs at Hahei on Coromandel Peninsula.*

Alpine panorama with Mount Cook and Mount Tasman, seen from the west coast.

to the mountains at Haast and takes us to the holiday center of Queenstown. From here, Highway 8 leads through the mountains to the east coast and the town of Dunedin with its Scottish heritage. Our journey ends at Christchurch, which is more closely associated with Englishness.

This journey is exceptional, not only for the stupendous and unique combination of mountain and coastal scenery on the west coat, but also for the vibrant remnants of a colonial past that are

### 4 Nelson – West coast – Queenstown – Dunedin – Christchurch (slightly over 1,500 kilometers / 930 miles)

Our longest trip takes us round almost the entire South Island.

*Always ready with a smile: in the Tasman National Park (below) and in Christchurch (bottom).*

Why only almost? Because many tourists arriving at the ferry harbor of Picton tend to leave the island again from Christchurch's airport. This route includes many of the famously beautiful island's sights – starting with the abundantly blossoming Nelson, a little town that was more or less bankrupt in 1844 and was saved by the arrival of German immigrants. South of Nelson, the road continues over hilly countryside down to the west coast, a small strip of land at the foot of the long ridge of mountains known as the New Zealand Alps.

Clouds tend to rain off their moisture here, creating a climate that has led to the growth of a rain forest that lines the coastal road with massive fern trees. Two glaciers come down almost as far as the shore along the middle stretch of road, and above them, mountains rise up to a height of 3,755 meters (12,320 feet). The road turns off in-

Isel House in Nelson's Isel Gardens has a typically Victorian demeanor.

## SOUTH ISLAND

Farewell Spit
Marlborough Sounds
Golden Bay
ABEL TASMAN NATIONAL PARK
Abel Tasman Track
Tasman Bay
Heaphy Track
Picton
Nelson
Havelock
Blenheim
Cook Strait
[4]
Wairau
Westport
Lake Rotoiti
Lake Rotoroa
Mt. Travers 2338
Kaikoura
Cape Foulwind
Charleston
NELSON LAKES NATIONAL PARK
PAPAROA NATIONAL PARK
Pancake Rocks ★
Punakaiki
Lake Summer
Tasman Sea
Greymouth
Shantytown ★
Lake Brunner
ARTHUR'S PASS NATIONAL PARK
Waipara
Hokitika
[4]
Arthur's Pass 920
Ross
[5]
Pegasus Bay
Christchurch
BANKS PENINSULA
Southern Alps
Mt. Hutt 2226
Canterbury Plains
Lake Ellesmere
Akaroa
Franz Josef Glacier
Methven
Mt. Tasman 3497
MT. COOK NAT. PARK
Fox Glacier 3754
Mt. Cook (Aorangi)
WESTLAND NAT. PARK
Lake Tekapo
Timaru
Hermitage
[4]
Mackenzieland
Lake Pukaki
Lake Benmore
Haast
MT. ASPIRING NATIONAL PARK
Lake Ohau
Omarama
Lake Hawea
Mt. Aspiring 3027
Pukeuri Junction
Lake Wanaka
Oamaru
Wanaka
Moeraki
Milford Sound
Milford Sound
Cromwell
OTAGO
1692 Mitre Peak
Queenstown
Taiaroa Head OTAGO
Lake Wakatipu
Dunedin
Te Anau
[4]
Lake Te Anau
Milton
Lumsden
FJORDLAND NATIONAL PARK
Manapouri
PAZIFIC OCEAN
Invercargill
Bluff
RUAPUKE
Foveaux Strait
Halfmoon Bay (Oban)
STEWART ISLAND

N
0    50 km
0    31 miles

*Mount Cook on Lake Pukaki (left).*

---

manifest on the east coast. The trip from Nelson to Christchurch shows you all that is characteristic of South Island.

## 5. Christchurch – Greymouth in the TranzAlpine (250 kilometers / 150 miles)

The road over Arthur's Pass in the New Zealand Alps was blasted through rock and wilderness to create access to the west coast's gold reserves. Although the original hairpin curves have been straightened out, taking the Tranz Alpine train through this stretch of country remains a comfortable alternative to driving.

Despite being only 250 kilometers (150 miles) long, the trip between Christchurch and Greymouth is one of the world's greatest train-rides – providing spectacular views of a cross-section of South Island's topography. The first part of the trip takes passengers through the Canterbury Plains chugging through highland valleys and over viaducts through scenery familiar to many from countless New Zealand posters that show white sheep dotted on green pastures in front of snow-capped mountains.

The train stops not far from the pass and many passengers dismount to start out on hikes through the national park. The weather up here can serve to remind visitors that New Zealand's west coast belongs to the country's

*Endless vistas: the TranzAlpine-Express at Lake Brunner.*

rainy regions. If it does start pouring cats and dogs, ask the locals in Arthur's Pass Store for an assessment of the weather conditions: they might forecast a couple of showers, in which case you can take shelter for an hour before starting off. If it looks like continuous rain, it's probably better to get back on the train and continue on westwards.

After having crossed the pass at an altitude of 924 meters (3,031 feet), the route begins winding downward along the Grey River and past Lake Brunner to the Tasman See, reaching Greymouth after four-and-a-half hours. There is not much in the former gold-mining town to remind visitors of this heritage, but Shantytown down the road – specially constructed to give tourists an idea of the gold-digging era – more than makes up for this deficit.

151

# Jet Set

## It's the only way to fly

The canyons of Shotover River near Queenstown are never quiet: the rushing or roaring of mountain rivers takes care of that. But sometimes even these natural noises are drowned out by the shrill shrieks of tourists chasing through the canyons in a

jet boat, jumping round corners like rabbits, almost turning on the spot. Jet boats are a sure-fire way to get the adrenalin pumping whether it's here in New Zealand or any place in the world where there are fast, shal-

low waters in which boats with a propeller would be liable to get grounded. Since 1954, the New Zealander Bill Hamilton has the patent on these boats, which suck up water on their underside, pressing it out again at the rear end of the boat just above the surface of the water.

There were earlier versions, none of which, however, stood the test of practical experience. Bill Hamilton convinced the entire world market with his model when he was the first to zip through the Grand Canyon in 1960. Now knighted and known as Sir William, the discoverer of the jet boat refuses to take any credit for his achievement: "All the glory belongs to a guy called Archimedes."

*Inside and out: a jet boat on Shotover River near Queenstown.*

country measures 1,600 kilometers (1,000 miles). It has a breadth of about 450 kilometers (280 miles) at its widest point. The island state is situated in the South Pacific and is separated from Australia by about 1,600 kilometers (1,000 miles) of Tasman Sea. Tokyo and San Francisco are both about 10,000 kilometers (around 6,200 miles) away. From a geographical point of view, New Zealand's closest neighbors are New Caledonia, the Fiji Islands, and Tonga. New Zealand is situated at the meeting point of two tectonic plates which led to the formation of the country's many mountain ranges either as a result of volcanic activity or as escarpments. The highest elevation is Mount Cook in the New Zealand Alps with an altitude of 3,757 meters (12,326 feet). New Zealand is subject to constant but generally mild earthquake and volcanic activity.

## Swimming

Since there are no dangerous animals on land in New Zealand, peril tends to lurk mainly in the ocean. Not so much in the form of sharks, which sometimes swim offshore, but as strong rip tides and currents. Most well-known beaches are patrolled by lifeguards. Swimming on unfrequented beaches should be undertaken with caution.

## Time zones

The time difference between the United Kingdom and New Zealand

is eleven hours (without taking daylight saving time into consideration). The time difference between New York/Los Angeles and Auckland is 16/19 hours respectively. New Zealand has its own daylight saving time between the months of October and March.

## Telephone

New Zealand's international dialing code is 0064. The national telephone grid is extensive. Popular tourist areas and holiday destinations also tend to have good cellular connection services.

## Tipping

Traditionally, the South Pacific does not expect tips to be given at the drop of a hat. On the other hand, once given, they are gratefully accepted instead of being firmly but politely rejected as used to be the custom here. Most Kiwis only give tips for special services but international hotels, up-market restaurants and taxis tend to

*Man can't do without his best friend: sheep-farmer in the Catlins.*

*Snail mail is still an alternative to email: letter boxes in rural New Zealand*

expect tips from tourists – generally to the tune of about 10% of the overall charge.

# Transport

Despite its low density population, New Zealand has a well developed transport network. This applies to air, train and bus traffic as well as to the roads that are generally well maintained for use by private cars. Signposting is generous and easy to follow.

Those not used to driving on the left-hand side of the road should give themselves a few days to adjust after arrival. Experience has proved that it's easier to get used to driving on the left in denser traffic where there's less chance of doing anything but following the flow of vehicles. All major car rental companies are represented in New Zealand, as well as some local providers such as EZY (www.ezy.co.nz) who tend to be slightly cheaper. Car renters must be at least 21 years of age: a national driver's license is all that's needed. Nowadays, deposits have

been replaced by a credit-card guarantee. In view of the distances waiting to be covered, it's as well to take a rental car with unlimited mileage unless you intend fly from one town to the next and only need a car for local trips. Some car rental companies will not allow you to take the car onto the other island, preferring an arrangement whereby renters leave their car upon departure from one island and pick up a new vehicle when they land on the other.

Many visitors to New Zealand travel around the islands in RVs or camper vans. These can be hired from several companies of which Kea Campers www.kea.co.nz) is one of the largest. Rental prices are based on the size of the campervan – between two and six beds – as well as the duration of the rental and seasonal variations. Those who want to explore the islands by motorbike but are reluctant to pay for the transport of their own machine can rent bikes in all shapes and sizes in Auckland from New Zealand Motorcycle Rentals (www.nubike.com). All

cost and time estimates for road travel should take account of the time needed to cross the Cook Straits between the islands – if such a crossing is planned as part of the itinerary. Prices and departure times are posted on the Internet under  ww.interislander.co.nz. New Zealand's tourist organization has included a time and distance chart on its internet site at www.newzealand.com under the heading "Transport."

New Zealand's Automobile Association (AA) provides a similar service under  www.aatravel.co.nz. The AA-site is a good source of information for motorized visitors. In addition to the three international airports in Auckland, Wellington, and Christchurch, regular services are also available to the regional airports in every larger town.

The railway no longer attracts many long-distance travelers from within New Zealand itself. As a consequence, rail services have

been geared to tourist needs. The railway company has even changed its name to suit its new image and is now called Tranz Scenic. Some of the trains now feature a panorama carriage with large windows. Visitors wishing to travel all four of the scenic routes are well advised to purchase a Scenic Rail Pass, either for one week or one month, including either one or two ferry crossings over Cook Straits (www.tranzscenic.co.nz). When the railway comes to the end of the line there is nearly always a bus to pick up passengers and take them onto more remote destinations. Each larger town is also accessible by bus. The two most important overland bus companies are Intercity Coaches (www.intercitycoach.co.nz) and Magic Bus (www.magicbus.co.nz). Bus services are especially geared to the needs of backpackers for whom they have several special offers that make traveling by bus even cheaper.

*A hostel built before concrete was discovered – Marlborough Hotel.*

Lake Tekapo lies at the foot of the southern Alps and is fed by glacier water.

# People, Places, Topics

*On White Island*

*Clowning around at the Wildfoods Festival.*

*Shantytown*

*Hooker Valley with Mount Cook (r.).*

*Maori once used these shells as a signalling horns.*

# Credits and Imprint

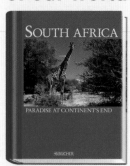
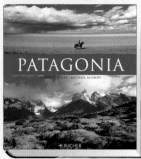
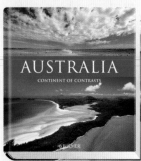

**The photographer:**
Clemens Emmler is an independent photographer and travel journalist. His work has been published widely in illustrated books, calendars, travel guides and travel magazines. He lives in Germany's Black Forest.

**The author:**
Klaus Viedebantt holds advanced degrees in folklore and is an experienced travel journalist and editor. In addition to authoring numerous travel books, he has worked for famous German publications, first at *Die Zeit* and now at the *Frankfurter Allgemeine Zeitung*. He lives in Frankfurt, Germany.

**Cover photos:**
Front cover: Mount Taranaki.
Back cover: Rotorua's green bowlers in front of Bath House.
S. 1: The art of Maori carving.
S. 3: Maoris and Pakehas (whites) celebrate Waitangi Day.

**Acknowledgements:**
The photographer wishes to extend special thanks to the following persons for their support:
Dawn & Mark Dowling, Jill Sutherland, Robert »Blue« Newport, Maren & Max Newport, David & Juliette Sutherland, Peter Vujcich, Dennis Buurman, Bruce Lilburn, Scott Lee, Nick Dobbyn, Dorien Vroom, Janelle Heall.

**Photo credits**
Interfoto, Munich: S. 18/19 o., 19 2. v.r.u.; 90 M., 90/91, 91 l.u.
dpa-picture alliance, Frankfurt am Main: 19 M. und u.r., 52/53;

All other photos were taken by Clemens Emmler, Simonswald

This work has been carefully researched by the author and kept up to date as well as checked by the publisher for coherence. However, the publishing house can assume no liability for the accuracy of the data contained herein.

We are always grateful for suggestions and advice. Please send your comments to:
C.J. Bucher Publishing,
Product Management
Innsbrucker Ring 15
81673 Munich
Germany
E-mail:
editorial@bucher-publishing.com
Homepage:
www.bucher-publishing.com

Translation: Eve Lucas, Berlin, Germany
Proofreading: Toby Skingsley, Munich, Germany
Graphic design: graphitecture book, Rosenheim
Cartography: www.karto-atelier.com
Astrid Fischer-Leitl, Munich, Germany

Product management for the German edition: Joachim Hellmuth
Product management for the English edition: Dr. Birgit Kneip
Graphic Design: BuchHaus Robert Gigler GmbH, Munich, Germany
Germany, revised by Wiebke Hengst, Ostfildern, Germany
Production: Bettina Schippel
Repro: Repro Ludwig, Zell am See, Austria
Printed by MKT Print, Ljubljana, Slowenia

**⊳B BUCHER**